Praise

A WALK THROUGH
THE PSALMS

PSALMS 91-120

ALEXA HESS

Study Suggestions

We believe that the Bible is true, trustworthy, and timeless and that it is vitally important for all believers. These study suggestions are intended to help you more effectively study Scripture as you seek to know and love God through His Word.

SUGGESTED STUDY TOOLS

- A Bible

- A double-spaced, printed copy of the Scripture passages that this study covers. You can use a website like *www.biblegateway.com* to copy the text of a passage and print out a double-spaced copy to be able to mark on easily

- A journal to write notes or prayers

- Pens, colored pencils, and highlighters

- A dictionary to look up unfamiliar words

HOW TO USE THIS STUDY

Begin your study time in prayer. Ask God to reveal Himself to you, to help you understand what you are reading, and to transform you with His Word (Psalm 119:18).

Before you read what is written in each day of the study itself, read the assigned passages of Scripture for that day. Use your double-spaced copy to circle, underline, highlight, draw arrows, and mark in any way you would like to help you dig deeper as you work through a passage.

Read the daily written content provided for the current study day.

Answer the questions that appear at the end of each study day.

The inductive method provides tools for deeper and more intentional Bible study. To study the Bible inductively, work through the steps below after reading background information on the book.

1   OBSERVATION & COMPREHENSION
Key question: What does the text say?

After reading the daily Scripture in its entirety at least once, begin working with smaller portions of the Scripture. Read a passage of Scripture repetitively, and then mark the following items in the text:

- Key or repeated words and ideas
- Key themes
- Transition words (Ex: therefore, but, because, if/then, likewise, etc.)
- Lists
- Comparisons and contrasts
- Commands
- Unfamiliar words (look these up in a dictionary)
- Questions you have about the text

2   INTERPRETATION
Key question: What does the text mean?

Once you have annotated the text, work through the following steps to help you interpret its meaning:

- Read the passage in other versions for a better understanding of the text.
- Read cross-references to help interpret Scripture with Scripture.
- Paraphrase or summarize the passage to check for understanding.
- Identify how the text reflects the metanarrative of Scripture, which is the story of creation, fall, redemption, and restoration.
- Read trustworthy commentaries if you need further insight into the meaning of the passage.

APPLICATION
(3) Key Question: How should the truth of this passage change me?

Bible study is not merely an intellectual pursuit. The truths about God, ourselves, and the gospel that we discover in Scripture should produce transformation in our hearts and lives. Answer the following questions as you consider what you have learned in your study:

- What attributes of God's character are revealed in the passage?

  Consider places where the text directly states the character of God, as well as how His character is revealed through His words and actions.

- What do I learn about myself in light of who God is?

  Consider how you fall short of God's character, how the text reveals your sin nature, and what it says about your new identity in Christ.

- How should this truth change me?

  A passage of Scripture may contain direct commands telling us what to do or warnings about sins to avoid in order to help us grow in holiness. Other times our application flows out of seeing ourselves in light of God's character. As we pray and reflect on how God is calling us to change in light of His Word, we should be asking questions like, "How should I pray for God to change my heart?" and "What practical steps can I take toward cultivating habits of holiness?"

THE ATTRIBUTES OF GOD

ETERNAL

God has no beginning
and no end. He always
was, always is,
and always will be.

HAB. 1:12 / REV. 1:8 / IS. 41:4

FAITHFUL

God is incapable of
anything but fidelity.
He is loyally devoted to
His plan and purpose.

2 TIM. 2:13 / DEUT. 7:9
HEB. 10:23

GOOD

God is pure; there is no
defilement in Him.
He is unable to sin, and
all He does is good.

GEN. 1:31 / PS. 34:8 / PS. 107:1

GRACIOUS

God is kind, giving
us gifts and benefits
we do not deserve.

2 KINGS 13:23 / PS. 145:8
IS. 30:18

HOLY

God is undefiled and
unable to be in the presence
of defilement. He is
sacred and set-apart.

REV. 4:8 / LEV. 19:2 / HAB. 1:13

INCOMPREHENSIBLE & TRANSCENDENT

God is high above and beyond
human understanding. He is
unable to be fully known.

PS. 145:3 / IS. 55:8-9
ROM. 11:33-36

IMMUTABLE

God does not change.
He is the same yesterday,
today, and tomorrow.

1 SAM. 15:29 / ROM. 11:29
JAMES 1:17

INFINITE

God is limitless. He exhibits
all of His attributes perfectly
and boundlessly.

ROM. 11:33-36 / IS. 40:28
PS. 147:5

JEALOUS

God is desirous of receiving
the praise and affection
He rightly deserves.

EX. 20:5 / DEUT. 4:23-24
JOSH. 24:19

JUST

God governs in
perfect justice. He acts in
accordance with justice.
In Him, there is no
wrongdoing or dishonesty.

IS. 61:8 / DEUT. 32:4 / PS. 146:7-9

LOVING

God is eternally, enduringly,
steadfastly loving and
affectionate. He does not
forsake or betray His
covenant love.

JN. 3:16 / EPH. 2:4-5 / 1 JN. 4:16

MERCIFUL

God is compassionate, withholding from us the wrath that we deserve.

TITUS 3:5 / PS. 25:10
LAM. 3:22-23

OMNIPOTENT

God is all-powerful; His strength is unlimited.

MAT. 19:26 / JOB 42:1-2
JER. 32:27

OMNIPRESENT

God is everywhere; His presence is near and permeating.

PROV. 15:3 / PS. 139:7-10
JER. 23:23-24

OMNISCIENT

God is all-knowing; there is nothing unknown to Him.

PS. 147:4 / I JN. 3:20
HEB. 4:13

PATIENT

God is long-suffering and enduring. He gives ample opportunity for people to turn toward Him.

ROM. 2:4 / 2 PET. 3:9 / PS. 86:15

SELF-EXISTENT

God was not created but exists by His power alone.

PS. 90:1-2 / JN. 1:4 / JN. 5:26

SELF-SUFFICIENT

God has no needs and depends on nothing, but everything depends on God.

IS. 40:28-31 / ACTS 17:24-25
PHIL. 4:19

SOVEREIGN

God governs over all things; He is in complete control.

COL. 1:17 / PS. 24:1-2
1 CHRON. 29:11-12

TRUTHFUL

God is our measurement of what is fact. By Him we are able to discern true and false.

JN. 3:33 / ROM. 1:25 / JN. 14:6

WISE

God is infinitely knowledgeable and is judicious with His knowledge.

IS. 46:9-10 / IS. 55:9 / PROV. 3:19

WRATHFUL

God stands in opposition to all that is evil. He enacts judgment according to His holiness, righteousness, and justice.

PS. 69:24 / JN. 3:36 / ROM. 1:18

TIMELINE OF SCRIPTURE

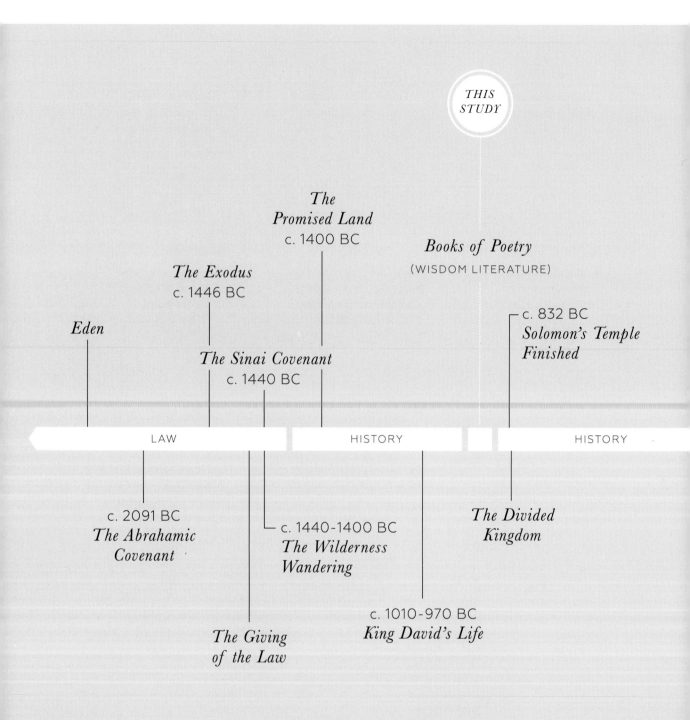

THIS
STUDY

The
Promised Land
c. 1400 BC

Books of Poetry
(WISDOM LITERATURE)

The Exodus
c. 1446 BC

c. 832 BC
Solomon's Temple
Finished

Eden

The Sinai Covenant
c. 1440 BC

LAW   HISTORY   HISTORY

c. 2091 BC
The Abrahamic
Covenant

c. 1440-1400 BC
The Wilderness
Wandering

The Divided
Kingdom

c. 1010-970 BC
King David's Life

The Giving
of the Law

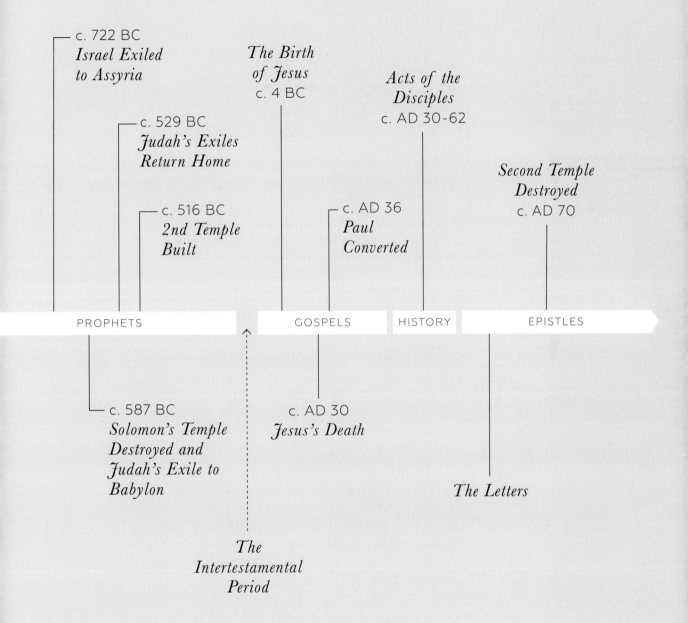

c. 722 BC
*Israel Exiled
to Assyria*

*The Birth
of Jesus*
c. 4 BC

*Acts of the
Disciples*
c. AD 30-62

c. 529 BC
*Judah's Exiles
Return Home*

*Second Temple
Destroyed*
c. AD 70

c. 516 BC
*2nd Temple
Built*

c. AD 36
*Paul
Converted*

PROPHETS   GOSPELS   HISTORY   EPISTLES

c. 587 BC
*Solomon's Temple
Destroyed and
Judah's Exile to
Babylon*

c. AD 30
Jesus's Death

The Letters

*The
Intertestamental
Period*

Creation

In the beginning, God created the universe. He made the world and everything in it. He created humans in His own image to be His representatives on the earth.

Fall

The first humans, Adam and Eve, disobeyed God by eating from the fruit of the Tree of Knowledge of Good and Evil. Their disobedience impacted the whole world. The punishment for sin is death, and because of Adam's original sin, all humans are sinful and condemned to death.

Redemption

God sent His Son to become a human and redeem His people. Jesus Christ lived a sinless life but died on the cross to pay the penalty for sin. He resurrected from the dead and ascended into heaven. All who put their faith in Jesus are saved from death and freely receive the gift of eternal life.

Restoration

One day, Jesus Christ will return again and restore all that sin destroyed. He will usher in a new heaven and new earth where all who trust in Him will live eternally with glorified bodies in the presence of God.

THESE PSALMS STIR OUR
AFFECTIONS FOR THE LORD
AND ENCOURAGE
US TO REMEMBER AND
rest in the mighty and holy
character of God.

Table of Contents

Introduction

Just as we can use a hymnal as our songbook for corporate worship, so was the book of Psalms the songbook for the Israelite people. The Israelites in the Old Testament used the book of Psalms as their songbook to worship God as they walked with Him and hoped in His covenantal promises. Psalms was written by numerous authors over the course of Israel's history and was likely compiled after Israel's exile. The book of Psalms is broken into five books, with the first half focused on lamentation and the second half focused on praise and the future messianic King. *Praise* is the fourth study in the *A Walk Through the Psalms* series, and it picks up where the *Seek* study left off by covering Psalms 91-120. These psalms primarily contain songs of worship and exhortations to worship God as King. While most of the psalms in Psalms 91-120 were written anonymously, some were penned by David, who was king over Israel.

While the book of Psalms was Israel's songbook, Psalms is our songbook too. The psalms in Psalms 91-120 give us words we can pray and sing to God in worship. These psalms stir our affections for the Lord and encourage us to remember and rest in the mighty and holy character of God. Psalms 91-120 also regularly point us to Jesus Christ, who is the fulfillment of the Psalms. As you journey through these thirty psalms, you will be reminded of the hope of the gospel and the greatness of God who is worthy of our praise.

THE PSALMS IN PSALMS 91-120

GIVE US WORDS WE CAN

pray and sing to God in worship.

God Most High

Even if we have not been in a dangerous situation, most of us have felt the desire to be safe. In a deeply broken world, we long for security and protection from tumultuous events. In this psalm, an anonymous psalmist writes encouragement for times of danger and fear. What makes this psalm comforting is the truth it brings about God amidst danger. It calls us to lift our eyes to our great God whose promise of protection calms our hearts.

Psalm 91 begins with a declaration by the psalmist, whose identity is unknown. He asserts that those who live under the protection of the Lord dwell within His shadow. In this first verse, the psalmist presents us with truths about God's character by using two names of God. First, God is the Most High. This means nothing is above the Lord; He is the ruler over all things. Second, God is the Almighty. Nothing matches the power and glory of the Lord. He is strong in might, and His power is inexhaustible. These two names of God encourage our hearts to rest in who God is. Our fears find comfort in the character of the Lord. In times of anxiety and fear, we need to remember our God is the Most High and the Almighty, and no earthly danger compares to His might.

In verse 2, the psalmist speaks about himself. He writes how the Lord is his refuge, fortress, and God. Knowing God is a refuge and a fortress, the psalmist trusts Him. But the psalmist does not keep this truth to himself. For the rest of the psalm, his language shifts from "me" to "you" as he speaks to his readers. The psalmist encourages us that the Lord will rescue us from the bird trap and the plague. The bird trap is figurative language describing physical situations that bring about fear and anguish. The plague, however, is not as physical. While we may see its effects upon a person, a plague is silent and invisible. By providing these two examples, the psalmist encourages us to see God's deliverance in both the seen and unseen.

In verse 4, the psalmist uses figurative language to describe the Lord as a large bird. A baby bird finds safety and comfort within the wings of its mother. In the same way, we can rest secure in God's protective hands. This promise continues in verses 5-8. In light of God's protection, there is nothing to fear. Verses 5-6 describe how God's protection never ceases. He protects us noon, night, and day. Verses 7-8 speak to the providence of the Lord. By continuing to use the example of a plague, the psalmist writes that while others may experience death, the one the Lord protects remains safe, untouched by the danger around him or her.

Verse 9 says the Lord protects the one who has made God their refuge and dwelling place. By acknowledging God is the Most High, we abandon all else and run to Him for our refuge. Worldly comforts promise protection but always fail to deliver. This is because earthly things are not designed to provide us lasting comfort and protection. Because God is the Most High and the Almighty, He is our true refuge.

In verses 10-13, the psalmist continues to promise protection from the Lord, using figurative language in verses 12-13. Strength from the Lord does not mean we will physically conquer all threats. But with the Lord, we can confidently handle anything that comes our way. It is also important to understand this psalm is not promising a life free from calamity. God's protection is intertwined with His providence. In our lives, we are not promised freedom from suffering and full protection from danger and disease. However, in moments of suffering, God's sovereign hand is not removed from us. While there are times when God will allow us to experience suffering, there are other times when He sovereignly keeps us protected. God's providence reminds us we are kept in His hands. Nothing can touch us without His permission.

The psalmist ends this psalm with six "I will" statements from the Lord. These promises are linked to the intimate relationship one has with the Lord. Verse 14 says God will deliver the one who has his heart set on Him, and God will protect him because he knows His name. These verses display the intimacy between God and the believer who trusts in Him. To have one's heart set on God means we worship Him and trust Him above all else. To know His name is to have a deep relationship. This moves us beyond simply knowing God intellectually to knowing Him personally. For those of us in Christ, this describes our relationship with God. All of these "I will" statements are promised to us. God promises to hear us when we call out to Him. He promises to be with us in times of trouble, and He promises His deliverance and protection. In moments of fear and hardship, we never have to wonder if God is present and helping us. With God, there are no unreliable claims—only sure promises.

Our protection from the Lord is rooted in our position in Christ. Without Christ, we do not have the promise of God's continual presence, provision, and protection. However, verse 16 tells us God will show us His salvation. While God will demonstrate this in physical ways in our day-to-day lives, God has ultimately shown us His salvation through Christ. The gospel teaches us we have been delivered from sin and death and are rescued from the punishment of our sins. We are satisfied with eternal life because of our salvation from Christ. His salvation brings us continual security. Because of Jesus, we can confidently say nothing will separate us from His love—even death itself (Romans 8:38). Even when calamity comes, we can rest knowing our fate is secure in Christ. We are forever protected in the hands of the Most High.

WITH GOD, THERE ARE NO UNRELIABLE CLAIMS——
only sure promises.

READ JOB 1:6-12. HOW DOES IT COMFORT YOU TO KNOW NOTHING
CAN TOUCH YOU, EVEN SATAN, WITHOUT GOD'S PERMISSION?

READ OVER THE SIX "I WILL" PROMISES IN PSALM 91:14-16. WHICH ONE
OF THESE RESONATES WITH YOU THE MOST? WHY?

HOW DOES THIS PSALM ENCOURAGE YOU TO WALK
CONFIDENTLY IN TIMES OF FEAR AND DANGER?

Magnificent Are Your Works

Today's psalm is a song for the Sabbath! The Sabbath was an important celebration for the Israelites. In fact, it was a command from God (Exodus 20:1-17). God instituted the Sabbath as a way to bring His people rest. On the seventh day, every person was to cease from their work. But this day was also a time to remember and rejoice over God's covenant with His people and His past work of deliverance through the exodus. Singing this song reminded the people of the Sabbath's purpose. This day was not about them; it was about the Lord.

From the start, we see the song emphasize praise to the Lord. In verses 1-2, the psalmist outlines three ways the Israelites should respond: give thanks to the Lord, sing praise to His name, and declare His faithfulness. Beginning the song in this way sets the tone for the rest of the song. This song is not celebrating what we have done but what the Lord has done. In verses 4-5, the people rejoice over what God has done and shout for joy over the works of His hands.

An improper way to celebrate the Sabbath would be to emphasize one's own works instead of God's. In our own lives, we can find it easy to become prideful over the things we do. This may even prevent us from resting as we place our time in our own hands. We can fall into the mentality that we are in charge of our lives. But we should not take credit for the work of our hands. God has given us the work we do, the skill to accomplish our work, and the strength to continue our work. When we emphasize our own work, we miss the many ways God has worked in our lives. He has done so much for us, and He is worthy to be praised.

While the wise and righteous acknowledge and praise God's works, the foolish and unrighteous do not. In verses 7-9, the psalmist describes the fate of the wicked. Unrighteous people may thrive for a moment, but their end is destruction. Verses 12-14 compare the unrighteous with the righteous. Unlike the unrighteous, the righteous continue to flourish and thrive. They are not like grass but like a strong palm or cedar tree. Even in their old age, they continue to remain healthy and bear fruit.

This comparison shows us the difference between the one who has a relationship with the Lord and the one who does not. A person who does not live for the Lord lives only for themselves. They pursue what they want and seem to flourish by their own means. But their flourishing is deceiving. In fact, without the Lord, no one can truly flourish. Their fate reveals the temporary nature of their flourishing. They may flourish in this life, but without the Lord, they are doomed to an eternity separated from Him.

WEEK I DAY 2 / 21

We can see this evident in our own day. Many people around us live, believing they are flourishing and thriving. They may appear successful and popular, always seeming to get what they want. We may even grow jealous of people like this. It can be easy to think, "How are they thriving while I'm struggling? How are sinful people succeeding while I'm suffering?"

The contrast between the grass and the palm tree deepens our understanding. Grass may sprout up quickly, but it dies quickly. A palm tree may grow slowly, but it stays strong and steady for many years. True flourishing is not determined by pace but by fruit. Sinful people may seem to be "winning," but the works of their hands are meaningless. As believers, our work is purposeful because we work for the Lord. We bear fruit for His glory. Verse 15 says our fruit declares to others, "The Lord is just; he is my rock, and there is no unrighteousness in him." What makes believers different is that we dedicate our lives to pointing others to Christ. We do not live for our glory but for the glory of the Lord. This is what it means to truly thrive.

Ultimately, our flourishing is rooted in our relationship with Christ. John 15 tells us that as believers, we are connected to the Vine, Jesus Christ. As His branches, we bear fruit, but only because we are connected to Him. Like a tree finds its source of life in its roots, so do we find our source of life through Christ. Our relationship with Him keeps us secure all the way into eternity. Even in the times we struggle to bear fruit, we can rest in the power of God working within us. Philippians 1:6 tells us, "I am sure of this, that he who started a good work in you will carry it on to completion until the day of Christ Jesus." When we feel like we are not flourishing, we can remember God is working within us. Sanctification may feel slow, but it always yields its reward. Because of our relationship with Christ and the power of the Holy Spirit within us, we will remain strong and steady in our faith. We can persevere in our faith because we have seen God's faithfulness in the past, we have His help in the present, and we know our future.

This psalm should encourage us to ask ourselves, "Am I continually praising God for what He has done? Am I pointing to the things I do or to what God has done and is doing through me?" Like a strong palm tree, we stand as witnesses to the strength of God within us. Our joy, even in moments of struggle, declares to others our reliance on the Lord. May we live in gratitude over the works of the Lord. He has done great things, is doing great things, and will do great things.

WE CAN PERSEVERE IN
OUR FAITH BECAUSE
WE HAVE SEEN
God's faithfulness
IN THE PAST.

HOW ARE YOU TEMPTED TO GLORIFY WHAT YOU DO INSTEAD OF WHAT GOD HAS DONE?

_____

HOW DOES PSALM 92 ENCOURAGE YOU IN TIMES WHEN SANCTIFICATION FEELS SLOW?

_____

TAKE A MOMENT TO REFLECT ON GOD'S FAITHFULNESS IN YOUR LIFE. LIST THREE WAYS
GOD HAS BEEN FAITHFUL TO YOU, AND THANK HIM FOR WHAT HE HAS DONE.

_____

The Lord Reigns

Psalm 93 opens with the words, "The Lord reigns!" In today's Western culture, we are not very familiar with the idea of someone reigning. Unless we keep up with the royal family in England or read fiction novels, the language of a sovereign or a king is not as common as it once was. However, this psalm begins a series of psalms about God being the king, declaring God as both a sovereign and sovereign over all things.

A sovereign is described as being a supreme ruler. To be sovereign means to possess ultimate power. When we talk about the sovereignty of God, we refer to His total control over all things. God's sovereignty is usually paired with His providence, meaning He divinely orchestrates time and events. In Psalm 93, the psalmist praises God for both His majesty and eternality.

Verse 1 proclaims God's majesty. The psalmist says that the Lord is "robed in majesty" and "enveloped in strength." A king's robe would symbolize His authority. This picture of God being robed describes His great authority, majesty, and strength. He is like a grand king clothed in robes of the finest quality. He is our great King—mighty and magnificent.

Verse 2 highlights God's eternality. God's throne was not created with the rest of creation. God has always existed, which means His throne has always existed. He surpasses any earthly king, for God has reigned for all of eternity. This, too, speaks to God's sovereignty. Nothing can shake the world, for God holds it in His hands. This can be hard for us to understand since we often feel the chaos and confusion of this fallen world. When natural disaster strikes or tumultuous events occur, we can feel as if our world is a snow globe, shaken up with pieces falling all around. While there are times when the world is thrown into chaos, God still holds it all together in His hands. This gives us immense peace when tragedy strikes. We may feel shaken, but the God of the universe is not shaken. He holds all things together, even when things feel like they are falling apart.

Verses 3-4 speak directly to circumstances that make us feel shaken. The psalmist uses figurative language by comparing opposition to a rising flood. This could mean that during the penning of this psalm, Israel was facing attack from their enemies. Like a rising flood, their enemies might have been lifting their voices in jeers and taunts. Opposition from others can certainly feel like a raging flood pounding against us. But any form of suffering can also feel like a rising flood. In times of suffering, we can feel as if there are rising waters around us. At times, we can be pelted with waves of fear and anxiety.

Amidst the floodwaters of life, there is hope. Verse 4 tells us God is greater than the roar of a huge flood and mightier than the waves of the sea. What a comfort it is to know that the things that seem great to us are no match for the greatness of God. He is greater than any danger or suffering we may experience. In moments of fear and suffering, God's sovereignty washes over us—not like a raging flood but like a calming stream. We can rest in moments of opposition and suffering, knowing God is greater than anything we may face.

In verse 5, the psalmist focuses on the testimonies of God. The psalmist describes God's testimonies as completely reliable. God is a holy, sovereign, and eternal God. His holiness means He is set apart and sinless. No one is like Him, and nothing compares to Him.

He is sovereign, which means He controls all of creation. He is eternal, meaning He has no beginning or end. We can trust God's Word because His words are from the lips of a holy, sovereign, and eternal God. In moments when we doubt God's Word, we must remember who He is. The psalmist ends Psalm 93 by speaking to God's eternality once again. Holiness adorns God's house for all the days to come. God's house can refer to God's kingdom. Because God created all things, both heaven and earth are part of His kingdom. He has ruled for all of eternity, and He will continue to rule forever.

This psalm should move us to marvel at the greatness of God. Sometimes, it can be easy to forget how holy and majestic God truly is. In times of fear, we can focus on the floodwaters rather than the God who controls them. The disciples fell into this mentality in both Luke 8:22-25 and Matthew 14:22-33. In these instances, the disciples were overwhelmed with the storms around them, but Jesus demonstrated His authority over all things as He calmed the storm in Luke 8 and walked on the water in Matthew 14. Jesus is Lord over creation. There is nothing over which He does not have power or control. By dying on the cross and rising from the grave, Jesus declares His triumph over sin and death. Those in Christ have received deliverance from the powerful waters of sin.

While we will still experience the weight of sin and living in a broken world now, we can rejoice in the future deliverance to come. One day, Christ will return and set all things right. No more will there be floodwaters of sin and suffering, for Christ will wash them away forever. When this day comes, we will have the opportunity to kneel before Christ and declare His lordship (Philippians 2:9-11). But even now, we can rejoice in the lordship of Christ and the sovereignty of God. In every fearful and troubling circumstance, we can be comforted by the greatness of God. The Lord reigns!

IN EVERY FEARFUL AND TROUBLING CIRCUMSTANCE, WE CAN BE COMFORTED *by the greatness of God.*

WHAT TYPE OF "FLOOD" ARE YOU EXPERIENCING NOW? HOW CAN THIS PSALM
ENCOURAGE AND BRING YOU COMFORT AMID THIS FLOOD?

WHAT KEEPS YOU FROM TRUSTING GOD? HOW DOES GOD BEING SOVEREIGN
OVER ALL THINGS ENCOURAGE YOU TO TRUST HIM?

HOW DOES CHRIST'S FUTURE DELIVERANCE BRING YOU PEACE IN THE PRESENT?

Judge of the Earth

One mutual affinity our culture shares is a love for superhero movies. Over the years, we have seen a rise in movies designed to give fans the chance to watch their beloved superhero or superhero group. There is something we all love about watching justice. We cheer as the superhero defeats the villain when all hope seems lost. This desire in all of us points to the God we reflect. God is a God of justice. In Psalm 94, the psalmist proclaims the just character of God who enacts perfect justice on the earth.

From the beginning, the psalmist says God is a God of vengeance. Vengeance may sound cruel to us if we do not understand what it means. We can sometimes confuse revenge with vengeance. Revenge is an act of passion, but vengeance is an act of justice. It is just retribution for wrongdoing. The psalmist calls for God's vengeance in verse 2 by asking Him to rise up as the Judge of the earth and repay the wicked for their sins.

Referring to God as the Judge of the earth connects back to the psalm we looked at yesterday. Because God is a sovereign God, He controls the whole earth. If God controls the whole earth, He has the authority to judge the whole earth. In verses 3-6, the psalmist mourns the actions of the wicked. By asking the Lord, "How long?" it is apparent that the wicked seem to be getting away with their actions. They have poured out arrogant words, crushed God's people, oppressed God's heritage, and killed the widow, orphan, and sojourner. The psalmist cries out to God to put an end to these wicked people.

The fact that the wicked have not been stopped leads to their arrogance in verse 7. The wicked belittle the Lord by saying He does not pay attention to their actions. This causes the psalmist to mourn in verses 8-9. He questions God's justice. When confronted with injustice, we can find ourselves asking the same questions. It can appear as if the wicked are prospering and the oppressed continue to be beaten down. If we forget God's sovereignty, we can fall into hopelessness. But because God is sovereign *and* just, we can trust He will set things right. We do not serve a God who turns a blind eye to actions of injustice. He is not a God who closes His ears to the cries of His people. God sees, hears, and acts.

The psalmist affirms the sovereignty of God in verse 11. In their pride, the wicked believe God does not see their actions, but God knows every person's thoughts. To God, mankind's thoughts are futile or meaningless. This does not mean He does not care about our thoughts; it means the sinner's thoughts are unwise and unrighteous. The arrogance of the wicked causes pride, but God looks at them and sees their foolishness.

Because God knows the thoughts of man, He enacts justice fairly. When we try to take justice into our own hands, we can do so unwisely because we often do not fully understand the issue. As a result, we may act justly in our own eyes, but our actions end up being unwise or harmful. But God is different. He knows everything, which means He knows exactly what is right in every decision. The Lord's justice gives us comfort and confidence. God will always do what is right.

In verses 14-15, the psalmist proclaims that though God's people are being oppressed, the Lord will not leave or abandon them. This brings immense courage and comfort in the moments we are the victims of injustice. Even when it feels like the enemy prevails, we can rest in knowing God will not abandon us. He will give us His strength and peace, and in due time, He will act.

In verse 16, the psalmist asks the rhetorical question, "Who takes a stand for me?" The answer is the Lord. Because God is just, we can have confidence knowing He advocates on our behalf. We are never alone in times of attack—the Lord is with us and fights for us. God's help gives us the strength to persevere under pressure or persecution. The psalmist writes in verses 18-19 that God has kept his foot from slipping, and God's comfort brings him joy. When our cares are heavy and our hearts are full of anxiety, God's comfort washes over us. He is our refuge and place of protection (Psalm 94:22).

Ultimately, we can find comfort in knowing God will act. In verses 20-21, the psalmist affirms God will not let injustice prevail. He does not side with the wicked or share His throne with corrupt people. As a God of justice, God will never let sin win. He will not allow injustice to reign. After all, He is the one who reigns. Even if His timing seems slow, verse 23 tells us God will enact His justice. The wicked will receive the punishment they deserve.

As believers, we can rest in times of injustice, knowing God will bring deliverance. Through His death and resurrection, Jesus declared victory over sin and death. Though it was not what we deserved, Jesus took on our punishment as sinners and set us free. One day, He will return to bring justice once and for all. Revelation 19:11-16 describes Christ returning with a rod of justice that will strike down the wicked. All unrepentant sinners will receive punishment for their wicked and evil acts. Through this justice, God will set all things right and make all things new (Revelation 21:4-5). God's future justice gives us hope to cling to in the present. In moments of tragedy and questioning, we can trust in the words of Romans 12:19, remembering vengeance belongs to the Lord. He is our great Judge who brings justice for His people.

God's help gives us the strength
TO PERSEVERE UNDER PRESSURE
OR PERSECUTION.

PSALM 94:12-13 TELLS US GOD'S DISCIPLINE GIVES HIS PEOPLE HAPPINESS AND RELIEF.
READ HEBREWS 12:5-11. HOW CAN YOU VIEW GOD'S DISCIPLINE IN YOUR LIFE AS
BEING FOR YOUR GOOD? WHAT DOES HIS DISCIPLINE PRODUCE?

HOW DOES THE FATE OF THE WICKED IN PSALM 94:23
ENCOURAGE YOU TO SHARE THE GOSPEL?

HOW DOES THIS PASSAGE ENCOURAGE YOU TO BE A PERSON WHO REFLECTS GOD'S
JUSTICE AND MERCY? IN WHAT WAYS CAN YOU ADVOCATE FOR JUSTICE WITHOUT
TAKING VENGEANCE INTO YOUR OWN HANDS?

Come, Let's Worship

It is always sweet to receive an invitation for something special like a wedding or birthday party. Invitations encourage us to join in the celebration of someone we love. In Psalm 95, the psalmist opens with an invitation for his readers to join him in worship. The psalmist says, "Come, let us shout joyfully to the Lord." The greatest invitation we can ever receive is one to worship the Lord.

The psalmist begins by inviting the reader to join in three different kinds of worship to the Lord (Psalm 95:1-2). He encourages his readers to shout joyfully to the Lord, shout triumphantly to the rock of our salvation, and shout triumphantly to Him in song. This particular type of shouting can refer to a military cry before going into battle, but it can also mean simply lifting one's voice in praise to God.

Why are we to praise God? The psalmist gives the reason in verses 3-5, starting with a list of three names of God. The first is "Lord"—or *Yahweh*—the personal and covenantal name of God. The second is "a great God," and the third is "a great king." The Lord is worthy to be praised because of who He is. He is a covenant-keeping God. He is greater than any earthly gods. He is a righteous and sovereign ruler. But He is also the creator of everything. By His hands, He formed the dry land and the peaks of mountains. He created everything; therefore, everything is in His hands. He is worthy to be praised for being the Creator and Sustainer of all things.

The psalmist gives an invitation to a different type of worship in verse 6. The previous invitation was to worship God through song, but this is an invitation to worship God by submitting to Him. The psalmist invites others to come and bow down before the Lord, kneeling before the Maker of all things. As believers, we declare worship, not only with our lips but with our bended knees. Bowing down before the Lord is a sign of submission and complete devotion to God. Some may appear to worship God while having a cold heart against Him and His Word. However, to worship God with our lips and not our lives is not true worship.

This was the problem for the religious leaders during Jesus's time. Jesus said in Matthew 15:8, "This people honors me with their lips, but their heart is far from me." As believers, we can easily fall into the same mentality. We can go through the motions when it comes to worshiping God. Perhaps we sing songs of praise in church on Sunday, but then we return to our week with no other thought of God. In doing so, our hearts and our lives do not match the words we speak.

The psalmist describes God as our Shepherd in verse 7. As His sheep, we are in His care. Following our Shepherd, we also submit to His authority and listen to His voice. In John 10, Jesus describes Himself as the Good Shepherd and says His sheep know and follow Him. But as believers, we do not always listen to Jesus's voice. This is why the psalmist shifts to a warning of improper worship in verses 7b-11. These verses are spoken by the voice of God, challenging and warning us by describing the account of the Israelites in Numbers 20. In this instance, the Israelites were not obedient to the Lord. Their hearts were not worshipful to Him. Instead of trusting the Lord, the Israelites tried and tested Him. Consequently, they were banned from the Promised Land and not allowed to enter God's rest.

If we want to worship the Lord with our lives, we must obey and listen to His Word. The Israelites did not listen to the voice of God leading them to the Promised Land. They tested God's faithfulness even though they saw God's continual provision and deliverance (Psalm 95:9). Their hearts were not submissive. Instead, their hearts went astray (Psalm 95:10). By their actions, they prevented themselves from experiencing abundant life in the Promised Land. As believers, we should be careful not to repeat the same mistakes. Turning away from the Lord keeps us from experiencing His rest. Rejecting God's voice and hardening our hearts against His Word keeps us from experiencing the abundant life He has given us through Christ. When we submit to God, listening and obeying His words, we experience a life of freedom and peace.

To live lives in complete worship, we must live in submission to Jesus Christ. When we turn away from Him and grow numb to the gospel, we live our lives for ourselves rather than Him. Meditating on the gospel keeps our hearts worshipful. In verse 1, the psalmist says we are to shout triumphantly to the rock of our salvation. The rock of our salvation is Jesus Christ. By His sacrifice on the cross, He has purchased salvation for those who trust in Him. He is our rock because salvation through Him is a steady and secure foundation. Our union with Christ means we belong to Him and nothing can take our salvation away.

As believers, we are called to live celebratory lives of worship in response to the gospel. If we find our hearts growing cold, we must warm them by going to God's Word. We need to read what Christ has done and then respond in worship to Him. As we worship God with our lives, we follow the psalmist by inviting others to come and worship Him, too. Our lives are testimonies to the salvation given through Christ. As we live worshipful lives, we say to others, "Come, worship this great God with me!" He is worthy to be praised, so let us dedicate our whole lives in worship to Him.

He is worthy to be praised,

SO LET US DEDICATE OUR WHOLE

LIVES IN WORSHIP TO HIM.

READ ROMANS 12:1. WHAT DOES IT MEAN TO BE A LIVING SACRIFICE?

HOW CAN YOU LIVE A WORSHIPFUL LIFE THIS WEEK?

HOW DOES THE GOSPEL KEEP OUR HEARTS WORSHIPFUL?

DO YOU STRUGGLE WITH OUTWARDLY BUT NOT INWARDLY WORSHIPING GOD?

WHAT NEEDS TO CHANGE SO YOU CAN WORSHIP GOD WITH ALL OF WHO YOU ARE?

Scripture Memory

IF THE LORD HAD NOT BEEN MY HELPER,
I WOULD SOON REST IN THE SILENCE OF
DEATH. IF I SAY, "MY FOOT IS SLIPPING,"
YOUR FAITHFUL LOVE WILL SUPPORT ME,
LORD. WHEN I AM FILLED WITH CARES,
YOUR COMFORT BRINGS ME JOY.

Psalm 94:17-19

Week One Reflection

SUMMARIZE THE MAIN POINTS FROM THIS WEEK'S SCRIPTURE READINGS.

WHAT DID YOU OBSERVE FROM THIS WEEK'S PASSAGES ABOUT GOD AND HIS CHARACTER?

WHAT DO THIS WEEK'S PASSAGES REVEAL ABOUT THE CONDITION OF MANKIND AND YOURSELF?

Read Psalms 91-95

HOW DO THESE PASSAGES POINT TO THE GOSPEL?

HOW SHOULD YOU RESPOND TO THESE PASSAGES? WHAT SPECIFIC
ACTION STEPS CAN YOU TAKE THIS WEEK TO APPLY THEM IN YOUR LIFE?

WRITE A PRAYER IN RESPONSE TO YOUR STUDY OF GOD'S WORD. ADORE GOD FOR WHO HE IS,
CONFESS SINS HE REVEALED IN YOUR OWN LIFE, ASK HIM TO EMPOWER YOU TO WALK IN OBE-
DIENCE, AND PRAY FOR ANYONE WHO COMES TO MIND AS YOU STUDY.

I'll Not Be Afraid (Psalm 91)

WILLIAM J. HENRY

I'll not be afraid for the terror by night,
Nor the arrow that flieth by day;
For the Lord whom I serve is my shield and my light,
He will guide and protect all the way.

REFRAIN:

I'll not be afraid, I'll not be afraid,
Where He leadeth I safely can go;
I will trust Him alway, both by night and by day,
He'll be with me forever, I know.

I'll not be afraid, though the stormy winds blow,
And the billows sweep over my soul;
He who calmeth the sea will protect me, I know,
And will lead me to heaven's bright goal.

REFRAIN

I'll not be afraid of the scorns of the world,
Nor to tell of God's wonderful love;
When from Satan's vile host fiery darts shall be hurled,
I'll be strengthened with grace from above.

REFRAIN

I'll not be afraid when the grave I shall see—
Just beyond its dark shadow is rest;
And the welcome of angels is waiting for me,
When I enter those realms of the blest.

Ascribe to the Lord

READ PSALM 96

In the last reading, we learned Psalm 95 is an invitation to worship the Lord. Psalm 96 expands on this invitation by calling us to bring this invitation to the nations. This psalm can be considered a missionary song. It was used in 1 Chronicles 16 when the Israelites brought the ark of the covenant—a tangible reminder of God's presence—into Jerusalem. In response to this occasion, the people burst forth in song and praise.

Like Psalm 95, the beginning of Psalm 96 focuses on singing to the Lord. However, the language used here indicates a song that everyone on earth is to sing. Verse 1 calls the whole earth to sing to the Lord, while verse 3 encourages us to declare God's glory among the nations and His wondrous works among all people. From these verses, we see that the gospel's good news should be spread over all the earth. God desires for all people groups, races, ethnicities, and nationalities to know Him. We see evidence of this in Matthew 28:19 when Jesus gave His disciples the Great Commission to make disciples of all nations. Later, in Revelation 7, John sees a multitude of people from every nation, tribe, people, and language before God's throne, declaring praise to Him. God is a God of the nations. As His people, we are called to bring the gospel to every nation and proclaim His glory among all people. This is our joy and responsibility as believers.

Verses 1-3 tell us how we can spread the news of God's glory. We can use our words not only for singing but for blessing His name, proclaiming His salvation, and declaring the wondrous things He has done in our lives. This is evangelism. As believers, evangelism may seem like a daunting task, but it does not have to be! It is as simple as sharing what Jesus has done for us in our everyday conversations. Joy over the gospel should overflow from our tongues. Every day, we have an opportunity to use our conversations with others to express gratitude for God and point to His acts of grace in our lives.

In verses 4-6, we see the reason for sharing God's glory. The psalmist writes how the Lord is great, highly praised, and feared above all gods, for all the gods of man are worthless. Unlike the gods of other religions, our God created the heavens and the earth. God deserves worship because He is the one true God. Spreading the gospel to the nations is important because other nations worship gods that do not exist—ultimately, they worship created items instead of the Creator. Proclaiming the gospel topples idols and points people to the one true God. As we declare the gospel to the nations, we orient their worship to the one true God who is great and worthy to be praised.

The psalmist continues to exhort our praise by calling us "to ascribe" to the Lord. Other translations use the word "give" in place of "ascribe." As believers, we are to give God the glory He deserves. We hurt our gospel witness when we do not give God the glory and praise He deserves. How we talk about God influences how others see God. Instead of looking like the world by pursuing idols, we joyfully proclaim "the Lord reigns" (Psalm 96:10). Honoring God above all things reveals our worship to Him alone. Our view of God impacts not only our lives but also others' belief in God. If we do not attribute the right things to God, we can believe something about God that is not true. As a result, God is not worshiped as He should be. And even worse, He can be defamed. As believers, we are to worship God with complete reverence. If we want the whole earth to tremble in awe over His greatness, we too must recognize and respond to His holiness. Our reverence should exemplify to others what true worship looks like.

We see the world's response to the greatness of God in verses 11-13. The psalmist uses figurative language to describe how all of creation praises the Lord in response to His glory. But these verses also point us to what will occur in the new heavens and earth. When God's judgment comes, through Jesus Christ, all sin and wickedness will be removed from the earth. What will remain is a people and creation who worship God wholeheartedly forever. Revelation 5:8-14 paints us a picture of what this will one day look like. In verse 13, John writes, "I heard every creature in heaven, on earth, under the earth, on the sea, and everything in them say, Blessing and honor and glory and power be to the one seated on the throne, and to the Lamb, forever and ever!" One day, His glory will fill the whole earth. But as we await this day, we have a job to do. As believers, our life's pursuit is to glorify God and make His name known.

Because God is a God of the nations, we are to be a people dedicated to bringing the gospel to the nations. We have an active role in sharing the gospel with every nation, tribe, people, and language. For some of us, this means traveling overseas to share the gospel, but there are people around us every day who need to hear the gospel, too. People from different cultures who have not heard the name of Jesus live in our neighborhoods and our cities. As believers, we are commissioned by Christ and equipped by the Spirit to make disciples of all nations. May we joyfully sing His song of salvation for the whole earth to hear.

IF WE WANT THE WHOLE EARTH
TO TREMBLE IN AWE OVER
HIS GREATNESS, WE TOO MUST
recognize and respond
to His holiness.

WHAT IS KEEPING YOU FROM SHARING THE GOSPEL WITH OTHERS?
HOW DOES THIS PSALM CHALLENGE AND ENCOURAGE YOU TO SHARE THE GOSPEL?

_____

READ ACTS 17:22-31. HOW DOES PAUL CALL OUT THE IDOLATRY OF THE PEOPLE?
HOW DOES HE CONTRAST THEIR FALSE GODS TO THE ONE TRUE GOD?

_____

ARE YOU GIVING GOD THE PRAISE HE DESERVES?
HOW CAN YOU POINT TO GOD'S GLORY BY THE WAY YOU SPEAK?

_____

Exalted Above All

Psalm 97 continues the series of psalms declaring the Lord as King. The psalmist begins the psalm with the resounding cry, "The Lord reigns!" The several past psalms have emphasized God's majesty, lordship, and sovereignty. In Psalm 97, these characteristics of God are shown again, but this time they are shown through a description of His revelation, or God's revealing of Himself. God is not a God who remains a stranger to His creation; He is a God who makes Himself known to the people of the earth.

Throughout the Old Testament, we read of God revealing Himself to mankind—whether through a burning bush, a vision, or the sound of His voice. The presence of the Lord is powerful, and every revelation of God in the Bible includes descriptions of His power. Verses 2-5 of this psalm use creative imagery to describe the power and holiness of the Lord. The psalmist writes how clouds and darkness surround Him, and fire goes before Him. His presence is like lightning that lights up the whole earth and causes the mountains to melt like wax.

If we close our eyes, we can visualize verses 2-5. We can see the swirling clouds, feel the heat of the fire, and hear the strike of lightning. These elements evoke in us awe and maybe even some fear. The Israelites experienced God's revelation in this way in Exodus 19:16-18. As God prepared to make His presence known on Mount Sinai, a thick cloud covered the mountain while thunder struck and lightning crossed the sky. Fire and smoke filled the air as God descended upon the mountain, and the people trembled in response. We might not have had this kind of encounter with God, but this does not mean our response should differ from the Israelites' response. Because God is an invisible God, we can sometimes minimize His power and His greatness. But one day, we will meet God face to face. We should not wait until that day to give Him the honor and reverence He deserves. The invisibility of God does not alter the totality of our worship. The holiness of God should bring us to our knees.

This psalm reveals how the revelation of God brings rejoicing for His people. In response to His glory, we proclaim His righteousness (Psalm 97:6). In contrast to the greatness of God, people see the meaninglessness of their idols. Verse 7 says those who worship idols will be put to shame, and all their gods must worship Him. The holiness of God reveals the futility of idols. If we were to place something we worship next to God, we would instantly see how worthless that item of worship truly is. But sometimes, we can elevate earthly things higher than God. We treat them as if they are greater and more powerful. We may not bow down to idols of gold, but we can bow down to other idols such as perfectionism, money, relationships, and success. God is the God Most High; therefore, He is greater than anything we tend to idolize and worship. When Christ returns to deliver justice upon the earth, all idols of worship will be disintegrated. Let us not cling to idols that will burn up; let us cling to the God who remains forever. May we humble ourselves before the holiness of God and place Him on the throne of our hearts.

As we await the day of Christ's return, we do not wait in despair but in hope. Verses 10-12 show what our response should be in light of what Scripture calls the Lord's Day—the day God will bring about judgment upon the earth. For those of us in Christ, we do not need to fear this day. The salvation we have received from Christ means we are rescued from God's wrath and judgment. We look to this day with hope and joy. As we wait, we have two promises of God onto which we can hold. The first is His perseverance. Verse 10 says God protects His faithful ones. Even though we may walk through difficulty in this life, we are protected in the hands of God.

Second, we have the hope of God's deliverance. Verse 10 continues to say God rescues us from the power of the wicked. As believers in Christ, we have already received deliverance from death. However, living in a broken world, we will experience persecution and spiritual attack. In these moments, we can cling to the truth of God's future deliverance. One day, He will return and remove all the strongholds of the earth. The grip of sin will be destroyed forever. In the darkness of the earth, believers have a light to cling to. Verse 11 says, "light dawns for the righteous." Light has dawned for believers because of Jesus Christ—the Light of the World. Jesus has rescued us from darkness and brought us into His marvelous light.

The perseverance and deliverance of God make believers glad, and we lift our voices in gratitude to God. Gladness and gratitude mark the life of the believer. Even though we wait for Christ to come and for God's revelation to be fully realized, there is joy in the waiting. But there is also work to do in the waiting. We respond to and reflect the holiness of God by being people of holiness ourselves. We do not have to look far to grow in holiness. We have been given God's Word, the revelation of Himself, to mold us. We have been given access to God in prayer through Christ to ask for His help in growing in godliness. We have been given the Holy Spirit who empowers and strengthens us to walk in holiness. We are well-equipped to live holy lives. May our worship and conduct reflect the holiness of our God.

WE ARE WELL-EQUIPPED TO LIVE HOLY LIVES.
MAY OUR WORSHIP AND CONDUCT
reflect the holiness of our God.

READ HEBREWS 12:18-29. WHAT SHOULD BE OUR RESPONSE
TO GOD IN LIGHT OF THESE VERSES?

_____

WHAT IDOLS ARE KEEPING YOU FROM WORSHIPING GOD WHOLEHEARTEDLY?
SURRENDER THESE IDOLS TO THE LORD NOW, AND ASK FOR THE SPIRIT TO
HELP YOU KEEP GOD ON THE THRONE OF YOUR HEART.

_____

HOW CAN YOU LIVE IN LIGHT OF THE FUTURE COMING OF CHRIST?

_____

Our God's Victory

READ PSALM 98

In the Book of Common Prayer, Psalm 98 is called the *Cantate Domino,* which means "O sing to the Lord," and it is nestled between the evening Old Testament reading and its New Testament fulfillment. Scholars believe the Israelites could have sung Psalm 98 after the exodus from Egypt or after their return from exile. Either way, this psalm is a song of victory in light of God's deliverance. It serves as a way to look back and rejoice in what God has done and to look forward to and rejoice in what God will do.

As the psalm begins, the psalmist rejoices over the works of the Lord. He calls for people to sing a new song in light of the wonders God has performed and the victory God has accomplished (verse 1). Whether a response to the exodus or the exile, both stories exemplify God's deliverance. The Israelites beheld God's work of deliverance as the Lord caused the waters of the Red Sea to part just in time for the Israelites to cross (Exodus 14:21-22). They also beheld God's work of deliverance by rescuing them from their persecution in exile and returning them to their land (Ezra 1:1-4). In either instance, God gave them victory, and for that, the people rejoice. In verse 3, the psalmist praises God for how He remembered His love and faithfulness to Israel. The language of love and faithfulness describes God's covenant with the people of Israel. A covenant is where two parties make binding promises to each other. God made several covenants with the Israelites throughout the years. However, the Israelites struggled to keep their covenants with God. Still, we see God continuing to uphold His covenant throughout the Old Testament, even when Israel disobeyed. Even through difficulty, God continues to rescue His people and fulfill His covenant promises. We serve a God whose faithfulness and steadfast love follow us all the days of our lives.

As believers in Christ, we have seen God's love and faithfulness through His Son, Jesus. God not only kept all of His covenant promises; He also fulfilled all of His covenant promises through Christ. By His great love and faithfulness, God gave His Son as a sacrifice for mankind. The salvation and deliverance the Israelites received points to the salvation and deliverance we ultimately receive through Jesus. As the Israelites worshiped God for His victory, Christians worship God for His victory through Christ. By dying on the cross and rising from the grave, Jesus proclaimed victory over sin and death. Those who come to faith in Christ share in His victory. Believers receive deliverance from punishment for their sins through Christ's forgiveness. They are rescued from death and given victory through Christ's salvation. The cross has won us victory.

In response to Christ's victory, we live as victorious people. What does this look like? We live in constant praise and gratitude to the Lord! We see the people's response to God's deliverance and victory in verses 4-8. The people burst forth with shouts of joy and triumph, strums of the lyre, and blasts of the trumpets and the ram's horns. In essence, they create a crescendo of praise to God—a concert dedicated to His glory.

As believers in Christ, God calls us to live lives of worship to Him. But can we honestly say we live this way consistently? Instead of praising God's promises, we often doubt God's promises. Instead of feeling victorious over our sin, we often feel defeated over our sin. Defeat does not define the Christian life—victory does. Therefore, despair does not define the Christian life—joy does.

If Jesus remained in the grave, we would have a reason to despair and feel defeated. Paul expresses this in 1 Corinthians 15:17 when he writes, "And if Christ has not been raised, your faith is worthless; you are still in your sins." But later in verse 57, Paul writes, "But thanks be to God, who gives us the victory through our Lord Jesus Christ!" We have hope to cling to because Christ has indeed risen from the grave. We live victoriously because we have been delivered from our sin, and one day we will witness Christ delivering the world from sin. As believers, we live with deliverance behind us and before us. Therefore, we have a choice to make. Are we going to live in defeat or victory?

The Israelites praised God for His past deliverance, but they also praised God for His future deliverance. In verse 9, the songs of the people and the joy of creation shift to focus on God's coming judgment. The people rejoice that God is coming to execute justice fairly and righteously. One day, God will judge the whole earth, saving the righteous but punishing the unrighteous. The whole earth will be cleansed from sin forever. In response, we will declare as believers, "Death has been swallowed up in victory. Where, death, is your victory? Where, death, is your sting?" (1 Corinthians 15:54-55).

This is not just a declaration for the future but one we can sing in the present. Christ is victorious over sin and death, and as followers of Christ, we are victorious over sin and death. May this present and future reality fuel our joy and endurance. Even in the difficulties of life, we can rejoice in God's faithfulness and deliverance. We are more than conquerors through Christ who loves us (Romans 8:37).

IN RESPONSE TO
CHRIST'S VICTORY,
WE LIVE AS
victorious people.

ARE YOU LIVING IN DEFEAT OR VICTORY? HOW DOES THIS
PASSAGE ENCOURAGE YOU TO LIVE VICTORIOUSLY?

———————————————————

WHEN YOU WALK THROUGH DIFFICULTY OR SUFFERING, HOW DO
CHRIST'S PRESENT AND FUTURE DELIVERANCE GIVE YOU HOPE?

———————————————————

SPEND SOME TIME IN PRAYER, REJOICING OVER WHAT CHRIST HAS DONE FOR YOU.
PRAISE GOD FOR HIS FAITHFULNESS AND LOVE DEMONSTRATED TO YOU THROUGH HIS SON.

———————————————————

He is Holy

Psalm 99 follows in the footsteps of Psalm 93 and 97 as its opening words declare, "The Lord reigns!" Continuing the collection of kingly psalms, Psalm 99 focuses on the holiness of the Lord. Lest the praises of the previous psalms cause people to emphasize God's works and not His nature, Psalm 99 emphasizes the holy character of the Lord. His holiness is to be recognized and revered.

Psalm 99 breaks into three sections, and each section declares God's holiness. For God to be holy means He is distinct and set apart. His holiness marks His perfect moral character and creates distance between His presence and sinful man. In comparison to the holiness of God, we always fall short. Therefore, God's holiness is not to be taken casually. He is not like us, and that is a reason to worship Him. Verses 1-2 capture God's holiness in two different locations.

First is God's throne. Verse 1 says God is enthroned between the cherubim or God's mighty angels. Revelation 4:8 describes these angels by saying, "Day and night they never stop, saying, Holy, holy, holy, Lord God, the Almighty, who was, who is, and who is to come." Angels surround God's great throne and continually sing of His holiness. Their song is for us as well. Every day, we should lift our voices to say, "Holy, holy, holy, is the Lord." The second location described is Zion or the city of Jerusalem. God's kingdom is both heaven and earth. His rule and reign cover the entirety of creation. The people's response to God's holiness in these verses is both to tremble and praise his name. Trembling in light of God's holiness is not to be afraid of Him; it is to be moved in awe of who He is. His holiness should move us to our knees as we worship the God who is exalted above all.

The next section highlights God's holy character. All of God's attributes connect with His holiness. He always acts in accordance with His holy character. Verse 4 describes the perfect justice of the Lord. If God was not a holy God, His justice would be flawed, but because God is holy, we can rest assured, knowing there is no imperfection in His justice. He always does what is right and fair. Once again, the people respond to God's character in praise and worship. He deserves for all people to bow before Him in worship.

In the last section, we see a holy God interact with His people. Mankind may be separated from God because of sin, but God does not remove Himself from His people. In verse 6, the psalmist lists three biblical figures who experienced intimacy with God: Moses, Aaron, and Samuel. These were all priests or prophets, meaning they served as a mediator for the people of Israel. As mediators, they received special access to God, and they were used as God's instruments to instruct the people of Israel. God's choice to reveal Himself and speak directly to man demonstrates His desire for intimacy with His creation. Our holy God wants to draw near to His people. What a gift of grace it is to serve a God who does not keep Himself at a distance.

For mankind to receive access to God, we must have a mediator. The gulf between sinful man and holy God is great, and there is no way for us to bridge this gap on our own. However, the gospel brings hope to sinners separated from God. Through Jesus's sacrifice on the cross, He bridged the gulf between man and God, bringing reconciliation for sinners. The forgiveness of our sins means our broken relationship with God is now mended through Jesus. We are now redeemed people, restored to our holy God. By His sacrifice, Christ has secured us access to God forever. Nothing separates us anymore, for the sin that once separated us was washed away by the blood of Jesus. Ephesians 2:13 says, "But now in Christ Jesus, you who were far away have been brought near by the blood of Christ."

Our response should be to reflect our holy God. The people of Israel were called to reflect God by being a holy people, set apart to declare His glory. As believers in Christ, we are called to do the same. First Peter 1:15-16 tells us, "But as the one who called you is holy, you also are to be holy in all your conduct; for it is written,

Be holy, because I am holy." The believer's lifelong pursuit is to reflect the holiness of God. All we say and do must look different from what the world says and does. It is a gift of grace to be a chosen race, a royal priesthood, and a holy nation set apart to proclaim the praises of our Lord and Savior (1 Peter 2:9).

To be holy people, we must remain in worship of our holy God. The true object of our worship is revealed in how we live our lives. We must follow the commands of the psalmist in Psalm 99 by exalting God above all things and living reverently in light of who He is and what He has done. The Holy Spirit helps us walk in holiness as He illuminates God's Word, convicts our heart of sin, and leads us to repentance. He helps us grow in our holiness as we undergo the process of sanctification, daily putting sin to death to grow in Christlikeness. As long as we are worshiping the Lord and walking with the Spirit, we can be confident we are growing in holiness. But even when we fall short, God's grace covers our shortcomings. As believers, Christ's forgiveness means nothing will ruin our access to God, even when we sin. We have intimacy with God that can never be taken away. The holy God is the Lord *our* God forevermore.

WE HAVE INTIMACY WITH GOD
THAT CAN NEVER BE TAKEN AWAY.
The holy God is the Lord
our God forevermore.

HOW DOES KNOWING YOU HAVE ETERNAL ACCESS TO GOD ENCOURAGE AND COMFORT YOU?
HOW CAN YOU APPRECIATE THE GIFT OF ACCESS TO GOD DAILY?

ARE YOU REVERING THE HOLINESS OF THE LORD OR APPROACHING HIS HOLINESS CASUALLY?
WHAT DOES IT LOOK LIKE TO RESPOND TO THE HOLINESS OF GOD IN YOUR LIFE?

HOW CAN YOU LIVE IN GRATITUDE OVER JESUS, YOUR MEDIATOR?
SPEND SOME TIME IN PRAYER THANKING HIM FOR THE ACCESS
TO GOD HE HAS GIVEN YOU THROUGH HIS SACRIFICE.

Give Thanks to Him

READ PSALM 100

Known as the "Jubilate," which means "O be joyful," Psalm 100 is a psalm of thanksgiving often used in liturgical worship. In liturgical worship, the congregation recites psalms or other readings of Scripture aloud. For some, this psalm may sound familiar as it is often read and sung during the Thanksgiving season. In Psalm 100, all the praise is directed to God alone. The repetition of the words "his" and "the Lord" attest to this. This psalm reminds us that we should live our lives in constant gratitude to the Lord. As believers, we should always have a thankful and joyful heart.

Psalm 100 lists the six following exhortations: let the whole earth shout triumphantly to the Lord; serve the Lord with gladness; come before Him with joyful songs; acknowledge that the Lord is God; enter His gates with thanksgiving and His courts with praise; give thanks to Him and bless His name. All of these exhortations point us to a form of worship.

The first two exhortations emphasize joy for the believer. The Christian life is a life of joy because of what Jesus has done. The good news of the gospel gives us joy everlasting. Because of this, we should be a singing people who always lift our voices to God. In light of who God is and what He has done, we are to serve Him with gladness (Psalm 100:2). What sets believers apart from the world is our attitude. There is a difference between serving the Lord with gladness and serving Him with grumbling. We are not to serve God out of obligation but obedience, not out of drudgery but delight. As followers of Christ, we should be a rejoicing people whose praise influences others and causes them to wonder about the source of our joy. The opposite occurs when we do not live joyfully and gratefully. Philippians 2:14-15 says, "Do everything without grumbling and arguing, so that you may be blameless and pure, children of God who are faultless in a crooked and perverted generation, among whom you shine like stars in the world." As we refrain from grumbling and continue rejoicing, we shine like stars. We are set apart from those who live with a negative attitude, always complaining and never satisfied. May this encourage and challenge us to take notice of our attitudes and words. The world is watching.

Verse 3 emphasizes our intimate relationship with the Lord. The verse calls us to acknowledge that the Lord is God. The word "acknowledge" means "to know, to have a firm understanding of who someone is." It is a gift of grace to know God personally and intimately. Knowing God changes everything. Growing in our intimacy with God and continuing to increase in our knowledge of Him transforms our hearts. As our theology grows, so do we as we live in response to the God we know and trust. Verse 3 also says it is God who made us. Because He made us, we belong to Him. How sweet it is to have such an intimate relationship with our Creator. We did not create ourselves, nor were we created by a chance encounter. We sit here today with breath in our lungs because our God crafted us. May we not take this lightly. The psalmist sees intimacy with God as a reason to rejoice, and so should we. We know the God who created us, and that is the highest joy. Verse 3 also illustrates God's relationship with His people by saying we are "the sheep of His pasture." This repeats similar language found in Psalm 95:7. As God's sheep, we are forever held in the hands of our Shepherd. He is always guiding and protecting us.

In response to His faithfulness, verses 4-5 remind us to rejoice in the Lord. Verse 5 says, "For the Lord is good, and his faithful love endures forever; his faithfulness, through all generations." We worship a faithful God whose faithfulness never relinquishes. His constant provision in our lives leads us to thanksgiving. We should always be thankful for what the Lord has done for us. Every day is a day of thanksgiving for the believer in Christ. There is always a reason to rejoice. But can we say we live in continual thanksgiving to the Lord? In the Old Testament, the Israelites failed to be thankful people. They grumbled and complained instead of recognizing and rejoicing in the provision of the Lord. Let us not follow in their footsteps. Our hearts turn cold and prideful when we do not live in gratitude. Without giving thanks to God, we take the credit for the blessings God has given. All we have been given is because of the grace of the Lord. We have done nothing to earn His goodness and faithfulness. May this humble our hearts and lift our voices in praise.

Ultimately, our salvation from Christ gives us a reason to rejoice. How could we not be a singing people in light of the gospel? We must let the reminder of the gospel, the hope of our salvation, and our intimate relationship with God fuel our praise and lead us to worshipful lives. By His great faithfulness and steadfast love, we are given new life through Jesus Christ. First Peter 1:8 tells us, "Though you have not seen him, you love him; though not seeing him now, you believe in him, and you rejoice with inexpressible and glorious joy, because you are receiving the goal of your faith, the salvation of your souls." May we daily remind ourselves of the gift of the gospel, and as we do so, let us lift our voices in praise to our great God.

BY HIS GREAT FAITHFULNESS
AND STEADFAST LOVE,
*we are given new life
through Jesus Christ.*

DO YOU SERVE THE LORD WITH GLADNESS OR GRUMBLING?
WHAT NEEDS TO CHANGE SO YOU CAN SERVE THE LORD MORE JOYFULLY?

_____

IS THERE ANYTHING KEEPING YOU FROM A THANKFUL HEART? WHAT ARE SOME THINGS
YOU NEED TO CONFESS TO THE LORD SO YOU CAN HAVE A GRATEFUL HEART?

_____

LIST THREE WAYS GOD HAS BEEN FAITHFUL TO YOU. SPEND SOME TIME IN PRAYER
THANKING THE LORD AND PRAISING HIM FOR HIS GREAT FAITHFULNESS.

_____

Scripture Memory

ENTER HIS GATES WITH THANKSGIVING

AND HIS COURTS WITH PRAISE.

GIVE THANKS TO HIM AND BLESS HIS NAME.

FOR THE LORD IS GOOD, AND HIS FAITHFUL

LOVE ENDURES FOREVER; HIS FAITHFULNESS,

THROUGH ALL GENERATIONS.

Psalm 100:4-5

Week Two Reflection

SUMMARIZE THE MAIN POINTS FROM THIS WEEK'S SCRIPTURE READINGS.

WHAT DID YOU OBSERVE FROM THIS WEEK'S PASSAGES ABOUT GOD AND HIS CHARACTER?

WHAT DO THIS WEEK'S PASSAGES REVEAL ABOUT THE CONDITION OF MANKIND AND YOURSELF?

Read Psalms 96-100

HOW DO THESE PASSAGES POINT TO THE GOSPEL?

HOW SHOULD YOU RESPOND TO THESE PASSAGES? WHAT SPECIFIC
ACTION STEPS CAN YOU TAKE THIS WEEK TO APPLY THEM IN YOUR LIFE?

WRITE A PRAYER IN RESPONSE TO YOUR STUDY OF GOD'S WORD. ADORE GOD FOR WHO HE IS,
CONFESS SINS HE REVEALED IN YOUR OWN LIFE, ASK HIM TO EMPOWER YOU TO WALK IN OBE-
DIENCE, AND PRAY FOR ANYONE WHO COMES TO MIND AS YOU STUDY.

All People That on Earth Do Dwell (Psalm 100)

WILLIAM KETHE

All people that on earth do dwell,
sing to the LORD with cheerful voice.
Serve Him with joy, His praises tell,
come now before Him and rejoice!

Know that the LORD is God indeed;
He formed us all without our aid.
We are the flock He surely feeds,
the sheep who by His hand were made.

O enter then His gates with joy,
within His courts His praise proclaim!
Let thankful songs your tongues employ.
O bless and magnify His name!

Because the LORD our God is good,
His mercy is forever sure.
His truth at all times stood
and shall from age to age endure.

The Way of Integrity

READ PSALM 101

David is the author of Psalm 101. As king of Israel and a man after God's heart, David desires to lead his kingdom righteously. The number of "I will" promises in this psalm seem to demonstrate David's deep desire to be a leader of integrity. David seems to take his authority as a king seriously as he serves under the authority of the Lord.

David's first two "I will" statements involve promises of worship to the Lord. In light of who God is, David says he will sing praises to Him and proclaim His faithfulness and justice. These two promises of praise connect to the following promises of obedience David makes. David desires to be a king of justice because He obeys the God of justice. He desires to be a faithful and righteous king because he serves a faithful and righteous God. David sets a precedent for what godly leadership looks like—to be a godly leader, one must obey and worship the Lord wholeheartedly.

David's "I will" statements in verses 2-4 reflect a desire to walk in holiness and integrity. To be a person of integrity is to be an honest person, someone who has strong moral principles and walks in moral uprightness. In these verses, David defines what this looks like: not letting anything worthless guide him, not practicing transgression, not having a devious heart, and not being involved in evil. David sets his eyes on the path of integrity and makes clear his desire to remain on that path. Recognizing integrity involves both his public and private life, David expresses his desire to have a heart of integrity, specifically in his home (verse 2). What we do behind closed doors matters. In fact, our private lives affect everyone around us, whether we realize it or not. We may think we can get away with sin when no one sees, but our God sees everything. Our sin will be found out, no matter how hard we try to keep it covered. Believers in Christ are to be people of integrity in both public and private spheres.

David also seems to understand that walking in integrity involves being led by the right things. In verse 3, David says he will not allow anything worthless to guide him. David is keen not to let sinful desires or sinful people guide him. If we, like David, do not want anything worthless to guide us, we need to allow our worthy God to guide us. When we let the Word of God guide us, we will remain on the path of integrity. As we read and obey God's Word, we are kept from our hearts growing devious and our actions falling into temptation. David also says he hates the practice of transgression and will not be involved with evil (verse 3). Though we will sin daily, as followers of Christ, we should seek to put sinful habits to death. Are any of our habits sinful? Are we watching or reading something sinful? Are we committing sinful acts? Like David, we should maintain our integrity by focusing on what is godly. Instead of following the world, we should keep our eyes fixed on following Christ and walking in obedience.

In verses 5-8, David shares his desire to surround himself with people of integrity. Using strong language, David explains he does not tolerate those who do not walk in integrity. As a godly leader, it seems David wants Israel to walk in righteousness and keep from evil. David does not tolerate those who have an arrogant heart instead of a pure heart, who slander their neighbor instead of loving their neighbor, and who have haughty eyes instead of humble eyes. Instead, David favors those who are faithful and walk in integrity. He invites the faithful to sit with him, but he prevents the wicked from entering his palace.

David teaches us that who we spend time with impacts our life. If we surround ourselves with arrogant people, we will find ourselves growing arrogant. If we surround ourselves with people who do wrong, we will be tempted to do wrong. To walk in faithfulness and integrity, we need to walk with people of faithfulness and integrity. We should surround ourselves with those who lead us closer to Christ. David's words in verse 7 reflect his words in verses 2-3. Not allowing wicked people in his palace allows him to cultivate a heart of integrity within his home. Surrounding himself with the right people keeps the wicked from leading him astray.

David's efforts to be a king of integrity are admirable. However, David fails to maintain these efforts. In 2 Samuel 11, David goes against his vow in verses 2-4 when he uses his position of power to take a woman into his home and sleep with her. His private decision turns public as he eventually murders to cover up his sin. David's failure to be a king of integrity points to our need for the true King of integrity, Jesus Christ. Unlike all the rulers in the Bible, Jesus is the only One who remained sinless and perfectly obedient to the Lord. He always spoke and walked by truth.

When we look at ourselves, we realize we, like David, fail to be people of integrity. Even in our best pursuits, we fall into sin. However, through the good news of the gospel, we have received forgiveness for our sins. Those who trust in Jesus receive grace for failing to walk in integrity. Not only this, but believers in Christ receive help walking in integrity. The Holy Spirit daily helps us walk in holiness by keeping our eyes on Christ and convicting us when we sin. Even though David failed to keep his promises, we should still seek these desires. Let us strive to be people of integrity, allowing the Word of God to guide us on the path of righteousness.

Let us strive to be people of integrity,
ALLOWING THE WORD OF GOD TO GUIDE US
ON THE PATH OF RIGHTEOUSNESS.

LOOKING BACK THROUGH DAVID'S "I WILL" PROMISES, WHICH PROMISE DO YOU SEE YOURSELF
CURRENTLY PURSUING? WHICH PROMISE DO YOU NEED TO PURSUE MORE IN YOUR LIFE?

_____

ARE YOU TRYING TO HIDE ANY PRIVATE SIN? CONFESS THIS SIN TO THE LORD.

_____

WHAT ARE SOME SINFUL THINGS AND SINFUL PEOPLE YOU ARE ALLOWING
TO INFLUENCE YOU? HOW CAN YOU TURN FROM THOSE THINGS AND
FOCUS ON CHRIST AND GOD'S WORD INSTEAD?

_____

Hope for Suffering

READ PSALM 102

Most of the psalms we have covered so far have been joyful psalms. However, Psalm 102 shifts from praise to sorrow. The subheading of this psalms says, "A prayer of a suffering person who is weak and pours out his lament before the Lord." While the psalmist's specific situation is not stated, scholars believe this may be an Israelite in exile. Israel's exile resulted from their disobedience to the Lord, and it involved being removed from the land God gave them. Today's psalm teaches us what it looks like to pray to God amidst suffering and how to find hope even when all seems lost.

The subheading describes the psalmist's lament. A lament is a type of prayer that expresses deep sorrow and grief. It usually involves crying out to the Lord and asking Him to act. We see evidence of this in verses 1-2. The psalmist asks four things from God: to hear his prayer and his cry, not to hide His face from him, to listen to him, and to answer him quickly when he calls. Many of us can identify with these prayers. Almost all of us have experienced times when we feel like God is distant and our prayers hit the ceiling. But the fact that the psalmist is praying to God reveals his belief that God hears and answers him. The psalmist teaches us that we must never stop praying when we are suffering. God may feel far from us, but He is always near. Times of suffering should move us closer to the Lord, not away from Him.

Verses 3-11 teach us it is good to honestly share our struggles with the Lord. The psalmist uses figurative language to describe every aspect of his suffering to the Lord. He writes in verse 3 how his days feel fleeting and how his body is physically suffering. In verse 4, he describes how his heart feels dried up like withered grass. In verses 4-5, he says his suffering is so great he cannot eat. In verses 6-7, he describes feeling restless and alone. He is attacked and mocked by enemies in verse 8, and his grief is great in verse 9. He even says he feels like the Lord has tossed him aside in verse 10. As we look at each of these expressions of sorrow, we have likely experienced at least one or two of these feelings ourselves. The psalmist's expressions show us life is not devoid of suffering. In fact, including this psalm of sorrow, among other psalms of joy, reveals the reality of life. Not everything in life is easy and joyful. In a broken world, we experience pain, grief, and suffering. In these moments, it is good to pray honestly to God. Brokenness does not surprise the Lord.

However, we see a turning point in verse 12 as the psalmist moves from sorrow to proclaiming the character of God. This shift teaches us another important lesson of lament: lament always involves a turning point. As believers, we are to pray honestly to the Lord, but we should not end our prayers here. Our prayers ought to include a turning point that declares the truth of who God is. Doing so, our eyes lift up in hope instead of down in despair. Even in deep suffering, we can cling to the character of God. In verses 12-22, the psalmist finds hope in both God's character and future work. In verse 12, he writes God is enthroned forever. Even in times of darkness and despair, God never stops reigning. He is in control of all things, and He divinely orchestrates every aspect of our lives —even our suffering.

The psalmist looks ahead in verses 13-18 with multiple "He will" statements. The psalmist can remain hopeful because he knows God will have compassion and rebuild Zion in His timing. He knows God will pay attention to the prayers of the destitute. He knows God does not turn a blind eye but looks down, hears the groans of His people, and sets prisoners free. If the psalmist is indeed in the context of Israel's exile, he is finding hope in God's future deliverance. He trusts that God will restore Israel. Even if he does not live to see this deliverance, he knows the Israelites will one day be restored.

The psalmist's focus on what God will do in the future gives him hope in the present. In times of suffering, we can find hope in the promises of the Lord. When we find ourselves in difficult circumstances, we can trust who God is and what He will do.

God is a God of deliverance. He does not allow suffering to remain forever. Even if His timing seems slow, God will bring deliverance and restoration in His perfect timing. By setting our eyes on what is to come, we rest knowing our suffering is not in vain. Suffering is never meaningless, even if it feels meaningless to us. Even when we cannot explain or understand our suffering, we can trust God is working.

As believers, our ultimate hope in suffering is Jesus Christ. Psalm 102:25-27 is quoted in Hebrews 1:10-12 to praise Jesus Christ. While the psalmist is looking ahead to the deliverance of Israel, Hebrews 1:10-12 shows us how Psalm 102 also points to God's deliverance through Jesus Christ. In moments of suffering, we can look ahead to Christ's future deliverance and find endurance and perseverance for the present. Knowing one day Jesus will set all things right gives us hope in our waiting. By looking at what is to come, we see our suffering is not for nothing. He will restore us and deliver us. Because of the blood of Jesus, we have been delivered from the punishment of our sins. We can have hope in the present, knowing our salvation secures us an eternity with God. May this psalm encourage us to be honest and hopeful in prayer. God knows our pain, and He promises to set all things right.

GOD KNOWS OUR PAIN, AND
He promises to set all things right.

ARE YOU HONEST WITH GOD IN PRAYER? HOW DOES THIS PSALM
ENCOURAGE YOU TO SPEAK HONESTLY TO THE LORD?

_____

WHY IS IT IMPORTANT TO HAVE A TURNING POINT IN OUR LAMENTATION? WHAT PROMISES
OF THE LORD CAN YOU USE AS TURNING POINTS IN YOUR OWN TIMES OF LAMENT?

_____

READ ROMANS 8:18. HOW DOES THIS VERSE
ENCOURAGE YOU IN MOMENTS OF SUFFERING?

_____

My Soul, Bless the Lord

READ PSALM 103

Psalm 103 is a psalm dedicated to blessing the Lord. David uses the word "bless" six times to emphasize praise to the Lord. In verses 1-2, David calls for his soul to bless the Lord. His desire to bless the Lord from the depths of his being teaches us what true worship looks like. Worship to the Lord should not be surface level but soul-deep.

In verse 2, David challenges himself and the readers of this psalm to bless the Lord, but he also challenges us not to forget the Lord's benefits. What are His benefits? David tells us in verses 3-7. God forgives iniquity, heals diseases, redeems life, supplies faithfulness and compassion, satisfies with good gifts, renews youth, executes just and righteous acts, and reveals His plans and ways to His people. What a list! David's encouragement to not forget the Lord's benefits teaches us to remember who God is daily and what He has done. How often do we remember the Lord's gifts? Sometimes the busyness of life can cause us to forget what God has done, or a troublesome situation can cause us to focus on the issue rather than God's past faithfulness. As believers, we should always remember and rejoice over what God has done. We should be diligent not to allow the cares of life to cloud the great works of the Lord. He has done so much for us.

Verses 8-12 call us to remember and rejoice over God's grace and forgiveness. We should be grateful to the Lord for all things but especially for our salvation. Verse 8 captures the essence of who God is. God is a God of grace and compassion. He is slow to anger and abounds in faithful love. This description of God's character, first found in Exodus 34:6, is the most repeated verse in the Bible—pointing us to the essence of who God truly is. He will not always accuse us or be angry with us forever. He has not punished us for our sins, and He has removed our transgressions as far as the east is from the west (verse 12). These are sure promises for the believer in Christ. Because Jesus took on God's wrath for us, God will never be angry with us. God will never deal with us according to our sins because Christ has already dealt with them on our behalf. God will never repay us according to our iniquities because Jesus has already paid the ultimate price. It is a gift of grace to never be punished for our sin, to never feel like God is holding our sin over us or using past sin against us.

Yet are we living as if God has done this for us? Are we resting in the grace and forgiveness we have been given? As believers, we can forget or sometimes even downplay God's grace. We can worry that God is displeased with us when we sin, or we can worry we will not be forgiven when we mess up. First John 1:9 tells us, "If we confess our sins, he is faithful and righteous to forgive us our sins and to cleanse us from all unrighteousness." Our salvation through Jesus gives us a secure life as believers.

Though we do not deserve God's grace, He has poured His grace over us through Jesus. There is great freedom for the believer in Christ. We can rest in the finished work of Christ, knowing we are eternally forgiven.

Verses 13-19 also give us security through the eternality of the Lord. In comparison to man, whose life is temporary, God's faithfulness lasts forever. His throne and kingdom remain eternal. When we doubt the Lord's faithfulness or forgiveness, we must look at His eternality. Because God is unchanging, we can know His promises are unchanging. Because God remains forever, His promises remain forever. Our salvation is held secure in the hands of an eternal God. From eternity to eternity, God remains faithful.

All of the Lord's works cause David to call all of creation to bless the Lord's name. God deserves the whole world to rejoice over who He is. Yet, the last verse closes in the same way the psalm opened. The soul of each believer is to praise God. Our soul-deep worship encourages those around us to participate in wholehearted worship as well. As we live our lives blessing the Lord, we point others to the great works He has done. As we rejoice over our salvation, we point others to the grace of Jesus Christ. All of this comes back to daily remembering the faithfulness of the Lord. There are hundreds of reasons to bless the Lord, and every day is an opportunity to praise Him. Let us bless the Lord with the depths of our souls.

GOD DESERVES THE WHOLE WORLD TO *rejoice over who He is.*

IS YOUR WORSHIP TO THE LORD SURFACE-LEVEL OR SOUL-DEEP?
WHAT NEEDS TO CHANGE SO YOUR DAILY WORSHIP REMAINS SOUL-DEEP?

_____

HOW DOES THIS PSALM ENCOURAGE YOU IN MOMENTS
WHEN YOU DOUBT GOD'S FORGIVENESS?

_____

READ OVER THE LIST OF GOD'S BENEFITS IN VERSES 3-12.
WHICH OF THE BENEFITS RESONATES WITH YOU THE MOST TODAY?
TAKE A MOMENT TO PRAY AND PRAISE GOD FOR WHAT HE HAS DONE.

_____

Our Great Creator

As humans, we can sometimes emphasize creation over the Creator. We can delight in the seasons changing but miss the One who orchestrates the seasons. We can rejoice over rain on a hot day but miss the One who caused the rain to fall. In Psalm 104, the psalmist continues blessing the Lord by praising God as the Creator. By drawing attention to God's creative hand, he encourages us to rejoice over the Creator of all things.

In verses 1-4, the psalmist speaks to God's majesty in relation to creation. Light is wrapped around the Lord like a robe. His palace in the heavens rests atop the clouds. Both the wind and fire are in His control and act as His servants. These verses call us to magnify the Creator. He is high and lifted up, sovereign over all. But God does not remain detached from His creation. In the following verses, we see how God is intimately involved in the creation He has designed. If these verses of this psalm sound familiar to us, it is because the psalmist is recounting the creation narrative in Genesis 1.

Verses 5-9 speak to when God brought order out of the chaotic waters that once covered the earth. By His mighty hand, He separated the waters and set them in their proper places. Verses 8-9 convey God's intentional design as the mountains and valleys were set in the place God established them, and the waters were set in a boundary that will never be crossed. Verses 10-13 show us how God uses the waters of the earth to provide for His creation. He uses streams of water to quench the thirst of animals. The mountains are watered by His hand, and birds make their home near streams. But God does not stop His provision with the animals. Verses 14-15 reveal how God has provided for mankind. God causes the grass to sprout and provides crops for man to cultivate and eat. He also provides wine, bread, and oil for humans to enjoy. God delights to give good gifts to His creation. He provides for our daily needs, but He also gives us fruits of creation that bring us joy. This great abundance from the Lord should cause us to lift our hands in praise to Him. We serve a Creator who delights in His creation.

The psalmist continues by describing other elements from the creation narrative. In verses 16-18, he describes how God provided homes for the animals to live. Verses 19-23 explain how God intentionally created the sun and moon to give us seasons. The rising and setting of the sun establish patterns for both animals and humans to follow. The rhythms of our lives are orchestrated by God's hand. The psalmist praises God in verse 24 for the countless works of His hands. In God's perfect wisdom, He has intentionally designed creation. As creator, God controls His creation. Verses 27-30 show the providential hand of

God. All of creation relies on God's provision. When God opens His hands, His creation is satisfied. But God also controls life and death. He creates life and takes life away. This providential work of God reflects the words of Job in Job 1:21: "The Lord gives, and the Lord takes away. Blessed be the name of the Lord."

God holds all things in His hands, and nothing is beyond His control. Therefore, everything we have and everything that happens to us is because of the Lord. There is security in the sovereignty of the Lord. The fact that God holds all things together should bring comfort to our hearts. God knows what we need, and He will always take care of us. Jesus taught this truth about the Lord in Matthew 6. Instead of worrying over what we need, Jesus calls us to trust in God because God already knows what we need. The providential hand of the Lord encourages us to surrender our striving. We do not need to work ourselves into a frenzy in fear that we will not be taken care of. We also do not need to rely on or take credit for the work of our hands. Our Creator has and will continue to take care of us.

This psalm encourages us to respond in three ways. The first is worship (verse 33). We should look at God's creation and praise Him for what He has created. We should praise God for the intentionality of His creative hand and for how He has uniquely created us. We should praise God for His provision and His sovereignty over creation. The second is meditation (verse 34). Every day, we should take time to notice and dwell on the works of God's hands. Let the birds of the air remind us that if God takes care of them, He will surely take care of us (Matthew 6:26). Let the growth of a flower remind us how God is growing us in the beautiful process of sanctification. Let creation point us back to the Creator. The third is hope (verse 35). Creation is beautiful but broken. Because of the fall, the world is not as God originally designed. The brokenness of creation should cause us to look ahead to when God will remove sin and restore the earth.

As we wait for the day creation will be made new, we can rejoice over how Christ has already made us new. In 2 Corinthians 5:17, we read, "Therefore, if anyone is in Christ, he is a new creation; the old has passed away, and see, the new has come!" The new self we have been given through Christ is a foretaste of the new creation to come. Praise God that He will not leave creation in its broken state. One day, He will restore the world completely. As we wait, let us do so with joy and hope. Our God is over us, with us, and for us.

WE CAN REJOICE OVER HOW
Christ has already made us new.

DO YOU FIND YOURSELF PRAISING CREATION OR THE CREATOR?
HOW DOES CREATION POINT YOU TO WORSHIP THE CREATOR?

HOW DOES GOD'S PROVIDENTIAL HAND COMFORT YOU?
HOW CAN YOU REST IN GOD'S SOVEREIGNTY IN TIMES OF WORRY?

HOW DOES BEING A NEW CREATION IN CHRIST ENCOURAGE
YOU IN THE BROKENNESS OF THIS WORLD?

A Heart of Remembrance

READ PSALM 105

Many people love learning about history. However, we do not have to be history buffs to appreciate the impact of history. History allows us to see how certain past events led us to where we are today. In Psalm 105, the psalmist praises God's faithfulness by taking a journey to the past. He takes a deep dive through Israel's history to praise God for the many ways He helped Israel. But what makes Israel's history so impactful for us to read is that it is our history. As believers, being part of God's family means we have ancestors who trace back to the nation of Israel. They are part of our story just as much as we are a part of their story. The Bible is a story of redemption, in which chapters of the past shape the way we see our present and our future. Most importantly, the story of redemption is authored by a faithful God. He deserves praise for how He has divinely orchestrated the story of His people.

The psalmist begins by commanding that people praise God for His past faithfulness. He writes that we should proclaim His deeds, tell about His wondrous works, and remember His works, wonders, and judgments (verses 1-6). In the hustle and bustle of life, it can be easy to forget all God has done for us. We tend to forget what is important when we get distracted or overwhelmed. However, remembering is a key component of the Christian life. While there is grace for our forgetfulness, we should daily seek to remember all God has done for us. The psalmist understood it was important for the nation of Israel to humble themselves by remembering God's past acts. We should do the same.

In the verses that follow, the psalmist starts from the beginning of Israel's history and recounts what God has done up to the present. In verses 7-15, the psalmist tells the story of Abraham and his descendants. He praises God for the covenant He made with Abraham to bring Israel to the Promised Land (Genesis 12:1-3). The psalmist also notes how God continued and confirmed this covenant with Abraham's descendants, Issac and Jacob. God is a God of covenantal promises. The covenants God made with His people demonstrate His great grace. These promises are promises of blessing fulfilled by a faithful God. He never forgets His covenants, and He will always see His promises through.

Verses 12-15 show God's dedication to protecting His people as He led them to the Promised Land. However, verses 16-22 take a turn as the psalmist recounts the story of Joseph. Israel's story seems grim as there is a famine in the land, and Joseph is sold into slavery (Genesis 37:12-36). Yet God proves Himself faithful as He uses Joseph's situation for good. Joseph helps Pharaoh and is promoted to the chief administrator (Genesis 41). These verses show us how God is faithful in times of suffering. Even in the unknown, we can trust God is moving and working. Chapters of our story may include suffering, but they are never wasted. God works all things, including the hard things, to accomplish His plan of redemption. We can rejoice over the truth that what the enemy intends for evil, God uses for our good (Genesis 50:20).

The psalmist continues in verses 23-36 to recount the story of Moses and the plagues (Exodus 7-11). The psalmist does not highlight Israel's slavery but highlights God's faithfulness as He powerfully used plagues to rescue the Israelites. Verses 37-41 describe God's great act of the exodus and the ways He protected and provided for the Israelites in the wilderness. Lastly, in verses 42-44, the psalmist writes how God remembered His promise to Abraham and fulfilled His promise by bringing the Israelites to the Promised Land. He triumphantly states in verse 45 that God did all of these things so Israel would worship and follow Him.

Psalm 105 encourages us to remember and recount God's faithfulness in our lives. We must remember God's faithfulness, whether we are on the mountain top or in the valley. Even in times of suffering, we can trust Him, knowing He works all things for His glory and our good. Most of all, He is worthy to be praised for bringing us His Son.

All of God's covenantal promises are fulfilled through Jesus Christ. God has shown us His unrelenting faithfulness by giving us salvation and new life through Christ. In the moments when we doubt the Lord or struggle to have faith, may we look to God's faithfulness through Jesus. As believers, we are written into the story of redemption because of Jesus Christ. In light of this truth, may we dedicate our lives in worship as we remember and rejoice over all God has done for us. Not only this, but we can rejoice because we know the end of the story. While the chapters in between may be difficult or uncertain, we can look ahead to the end when God will make all things new. As followers of Christ, our past, present, and future are held in the faithful hands of God.

AS FOLLOWERS OF CHRIST,

OUR PAST, PRESENT, AND FUTURE ARE

held in the faithful hands of God.

WHY IS IT IMPORTANT TO LOOK BACK TO WHAT GOD HAS DONE IN THE PAST?
HOW HAS GOD SHOWN HIS FAITHFULNESS TO YOU IN THE PAST?

_____

HOW DOES GOD'S FAITHFULNESS ENCOURAGE OUR WORSHIP AND OBEDIENCE TO HIM?

_____

HOW DOES THE TRUTH THAT GOD WORKS IN AND THROUGH SUFFERING
ENCOURAGE YOU IN YOUR OWN MOMENTS OF SUFFERING?

_____

Scripture Memory

FOR AS HIGH AS THE HEAVENS ARE ABOVE THE EARTH, SO GREAT IS HIS FAITHFUL LOVE TOWARD THOSE WHO FEAR HIM. AS FAR AS THE EAST IS FROM THE WEST, SO FAR HAS HE REMOVED OUR TRANSGRESSIONS FROM US.

Psalm 103:11-12

Week Three Reflection

SUMMARIZE THE MAIN POINTS FROM THIS WEEK'S SCRIPTURE READINGS.

WHAT DID YOU OBSERVE FROM THIS WEEK'S PASSAGES ABOUT GOD AND HIS CHARACTER?

WHAT DO THIS WEEK'S PASSAGES REVEAL ABOUT THE CONDITION OF MANKIND AND YOURSELF?

Read Psalms 101-105

HOW DO THESE PASSAGES POINT TO THE GOSPEL?

_____

HOW SHOULD YOU RESPOND TO THESE PASSAGES? WHAT SPECIFIC
ACTION STEPS CAN YOU TAKE THIS WEEK TO APPLY THEM IN YOUR LIFE?

_____

WRITE A PRAYER IN RESPONSE TO YOUR STUDY OF GOD'S WORD. ADORE GOD FOR WHO HE IS,
CONFESS SINS HE REVEALED IN YOUR OWN LIFE, ASK HIM TO EMPOWER YOU TO WALK IN OBE-
DIENCE, AND PRAY FOR ANYONE WHO COMES TO MIND AS YOU STUDY.

_____

O Worship the King (Psalm 104)

ROBERT GRANT

O worship the King all-glorious above,
O gratefully sing His power and His love:
our Shield and Defender, the Ancient of Days,
pavilioned in splendor and girded with praise.

O tell of His might and sing of His grace,
whose robe is the light, whose canopy space.
His chariots of wrath the deep thunderclouds form,
and dark is His path on the wings of the storm.

Your bountiful care, what tongue can recite?
It breathes in the air, it shines in the light;
it streams from the hills, it descends to the plain,
and sweetly distills in the dew and the rain.

Frail children of dust, and feeble as frail,
in you do we trust, nor find you to fail.
Your mercies, how tender, how firm to the end,
our Maker, Defender, Redeemer, and Friend!

O measureless Might, unchangeable Love,
whom angels delight to worship above!
Your ransomed creation, with glory ablaze,
in true adoration shall sing to your praise!

While Psalm 105 displayed a positive outlook on Israel's journey, Psalm 106 focuses on Israel's unfaithfulness to God. In Psalm 105, the psalmist left out Israel's actions to focus on the overwhelming faithfulness of the Lord. However, without knowing Israel's actions, we do not have a realistic understanding of Israel's past. History always contains the good and the bad. If we erase all the bad parts of history, we cannot accurately understand how past events shape the present. Not only this—seeing the ways humans fall short causes us to revel in God's faithfulness. Even in the unfaithfulness of man, God always remains faithful.

Before the psalmist recounts the negative parts of Israel's history, he continues to praise the Lord (verses 1-3). The psalmist also recognizes the grace of the Lord and anticipates God will bring salvation to Israel (verses 4-5). In verse 6, he openly confesses how Israel and its ancestors have sinned against God. The psalmist groups himself in with Israel by saying, "Both we and our fathers have sinned" (verse 6). He understands that the nation of Israel—himself included—has disobeyed God.

In the verses that follow, we see how Israel disobeyed the Lord. Similar to Psalm 105, Psalm 106 starts at a particular point in Israel's history and recounts the events leading up to the time of the author. Here, the psalmist begins with Israel at the Red Sea (verse 7). Even though Israel experienced God's mighty works through the plagues in Egypt, they still doubted Him. They forgot all He did for them and rebelled against Him during the exodus. Even still, God saved Israel, specifically for His name's sake. God used the mighty act of the exodus to proclaim His glory. After God delivered Israel from their slavery, they believed in God's promises and praised His name (verse 12).

However, the people's praise and belief were short-lived. Verses 13-22 recount all of Israel's shortcomings while in the wilderness. Israel forgot God's past faithfulness and did not listen to His commands. Overcome with hunger, they tested God in the wilderness instead of trusting Him. While God was gracious and provided food for them, He also sent a disease among them as punishment. Even still, the Israelites continued to disobey as some grew jealous of their leaders. Those people tried to overthrow Moses and Aaron, but God punished them with an earthquake and fire. One might think this visual display of punishment would keep the Israelites from disobeying, but sadly, this was not the case. In verses 19-23, Israel made a golden calf as their object of worship. They traded their worship of the one true God for the worship of a false god. The language in verse 20 is similar to the language used by Paul in Romans 1:22-23, which says, "Claiming to be wise, they became fools and exchanged the glory of the immortal God for images resembling mortal man, birds, four-footed animals, and reptiles." Here, Paul is speaking to the reality of all of mankind. As sinners, we naturally worship created things rather than the Creator. We may shake our heads at the Israelites, but we, too, have an idolatry problem. Our natural bent is to turn to things that gratify our own desires. We end up turning to and worshiping the things of this world, such as relationships, success, and materialism.

God almost destroys Israel for their disobedience, but Moses intercedes for the people, and God shows mercy on them. Yet, the Israelites continue to disobey. In verses 24-27, Israel refuses to go into the land God promised them. As a result, God punishes this generation by banning them from entering the land. However, the next generation continues to rebel as they align themselves with other gods and worship them. Again, God sends punishment upon the people, but a man named Phinehas intercedes for the people, and God relents. But the cycle of disobedience continues in verses 34-39 as the Israelites fail to obey God's command to remove all the people from the Promised Land. As a result, they mingle with the people in their land, and their idolatry problem grows. Horrifically, the Israelites partake in ritual sacrifices and prostitution. We learn in verses 40-43 how God hands Israel over to the other nations as a punishment. These other nations oppress Israel, but God shows grace to them by continuing to rescue them. Yet even in God's deliverance, the people rebel.

We see the reason for God's continued faithfulness in verse 45: He "remembered his covenant with them, and relented according to the abundance of his faithful love." Throughout Israel's apostasy, God remained faithful to His covenant promises. Man's disobedience does not stop the faithfulness of the Lord. God has shown us unrelenting faithfulness by giving us salvation, even in our rebellion (Ephesians 2:4-5). Not only this, but the intercession of people like Moses and Phinehas in this passage points us to the intercession of Christ. Though we did not deserve it, Jesus paid the sacrifice for our sins, satisfying the wrath of God. His grace covers our sins, and we are forgiven. Like the Israelites, our rebellion against God is great, but because of Jesus, we receive grace for our wayward hearts. As 2 Timothy 2:13 tells us, "if we are faithless, he remains faithful, for he cannot deny himself."

How comforting it is to know even when we fall short, God remains faithful to us. As believers, we are to live our lives in response to God's faithfulness. May the reminder of His great grace propel us to worship Him with all of who we are. Daily, we should be apt not to follow in the footsteps of the Israelites. Instead, we should be praising instead of complaining, trusting instead of doubting, and obeying instead of rebelling. But even in the moments we fail to be faithful, we have the sure reminder of God's unrelenting faithfulness.

EVEN WHEN WE FALL SHORT,
God remains faithful to us.

LOOKING BACK OVER THE DISOBEDIENCE OF ISRAEL, WHICH SINS OF THE PEOPLE DO YOU SEE YOURSELF STRUGGLING WITH? SOME EXAMPLES INCLUDE IDOLATRY, UNBELIEF, AND COMPLAINING, TO NAME A FEW. CONFESS THIS SIN, AND ASK FOR GOD'S HELP TO FIGHT AGAINST IT.

THE ISRAELITES' REBELLION WAS ROOTED IN THEIR UNBELIEF OF GOD.
HOW DOES UNBELIEF LEAD US AWAY FROM THE LORD?

HOW ARE YOU ENCOURAGED THAT EVEN WHEN YOU ARE UNFAITHFUL,
GOD REMAINS FAITHFUL TO YOU? HOW CAN YOU LIVE IN RESPONSE
TO GOD'S FAITHFULNESS IN YOUR DAY-TO-DAY LIFE?

Psalm 107 marks the first in Book V of the Psalms, yet this psalm is said to connect to psalms 105 and 106. The language of Psalm 107 describes thanksgiving after God's work of deliverance, alluding to God's restoration of Israel after their exile. This psalm also begins in the same way as Psalm 106, encouraging thanksgiving for God's enduring, faithful love (verse 1). Israel has witnessed the faithfulness of the Lord as He delivered them from the turmoil of exile. Now, they can proclaim His great redemption for all to hear.

Psalm 107 breaks into four different sections describing a specific situation and God's deliverance in that particular situation. These four situations are most likely four different ways of describing Israel's experience of exile. The hardship of exile is compared to being in a wilderness, in prison, in deep suffering, and in a vicious storm. Each situation is set up in a similar way. First, the psalmist describes the situation, and then the people cry out to God. God delivers them, and then the psalmist calls them to give thanks in light of that deliverance.

The first situation describes the Israelites being in the wilderness. Verses 4-5 describe how some were wandering with no city for refuge. They were hungry, thirsty, and close to death. After crying out to the Lord in their anguish, God rescued them from their distress by leading them to a city (verses 6-7). The psalmist calls for thanksgiving to the Lord, "For he has satisfied the thirsty and filled the hungry with good things" (verse 9). Without the saving work of Christ, sinners are in a wilderness, wandering with no satisfaction. Jesus is the Bread of Life and Living Water, the only One who can satisfy our hearts. Through His salvation, He rescues people from the wilderness of their sin and restores them with His waters of renewal. Unlike those who long for satisfaction to no avail, believers are satisfied forever by their relationship with Christ. Yet, we can still experience seasons of spiritual dryness. In these moments, we can cry out to the Lord, remind ourselves of God's faithfulness, and rest in His abundance and renewal.

The second situation describes being in a dark and gloomy prison. Verse 11 says this situation is caused by the people's rebellion. As a punishment for their disobedience, God broke their spirits and allowed them to experience hard labor (verse 12). After they cry out to the Lord, God saves them from their distress by bringing them out of darkness and breaking their chains (verses 13-14). In response to God's deliverance, the psalmist calls for thanksgiving to the Lord for breaking down the prison gates and cells (verse 16). This situation captures the deliverance sinners receive when they experience salvation. Without God, sinners are left in the dark. They are held captive to sin with no way of escape on their own. Through Jesus's sacrifice on the cross, His forgiveness releases those imprisoned to sin.

By His grace, He breaks our chains and sets us free. Jesus takes us out of darkness and into His marvelous light (1 Peter 2:9).

The third situation describes being in a state of suffering. Like the people in the second situation, verse 17 says these people are experiencing affliction because of their rebellion against the Lord. Their suffering is so deep that they resist food, bringing them to starvation (verse 18). After crying out to the Lord, God rescues them from their distress, sending His word that heals and rescues them (verse 19-20). In response to God's deliverance, the psalmist calls for thanksgiving, this time by offering sacrifices of thanksgiving and announcing God's works with shouts of joy (verses 21-22). Like being in the darkness of prison, sinners are in a state of suffering without God's salvation. Whether they realize it or not, refusing the gospel and remaining in their sin keeps them from the very thing they need to live. But in God's grace, He sent His Word, Jesus Christ, to open the eyes of blind sinners and bring them everlasting life (John 1:1-4). God gives us His Word, which provides sustenance for our lives. Even when we experience times of suffering, we can come to God's Word and find solace for our souls.

The fourth situation describes being in a storm. Verse 23 reveals how these people are tradesmen on the sea. While on their travels, they experience fierce winds and pounding waves (verse 25). With the fear of sinking, they cry out to God, and God stills the storm with His voice and leads them to a safe harbor (verse 28-29). In light of this deliverance, the psalmist calls for thanksgiving by encouraging Israel to exalt and praise God amidst all the people (verse 31-32). The storm in this situation reminds us of the storm the disciples experienced in Mark 4:35-41. The disciples became fearful over a storm that threatened their ship, but Jesus rebuked the storm, and the chaos subsided. Jesus is Lord over all creation, which means He has power over all things. Whatever seems powerful to us pales in comparison to the power of Christ. In times of fear, we can rest in the God who controls all things. In the storms of fear, God leads us to the safe harbor of His peace.

As the psalm closes, the psalmist recounts God's deliverance to Israel. Verses 33-35 describe how God brings both judgment and restoration. His restoration of Israel has caused them to prosper as God feeds them and makes their harvest flourish. The psalmist calls for the wise to pay attention and consider God's acts of faithful love (verse 43). We, too, are to do the same. God has shown His deliverance to us through His Son, Jesus. As redeemed people, we are to consider God's faithful works and proclaim His great name. We serve a God of deliverance whose faithful love endures forever.

IN THE STORMS OF FEAR,
GOD LEADS US TO THE
safe harbor of His peace.

READ COLOSSIANS 1:13-14. ACCORDING TO THIS PASSAGE, WHAT IS REDEMPTION?
WHY IS IT IMPORTANT TO REMEMBER CHRIST'S WORK OF REDEMPTION AND DELIVERANCE?

OF THE FOUR SITUATIONS DESCRIBED, IN WHICH SITUATION DO YOU FIND YOURSELF RIGHT
NOW? HOW DOES GOD PROVIDE DELIVERANCE FOR YOU THROUGH THIS SITUATION?

WHAT DOES IT LOOK LIKE TO PAY ATTENTION AND
CONSIDER GOD'S ACTS OF FAITHFUL LOVE?

With God, We Will Perform Valiantly

We all fight battles in this life—battles against temptation, perfectionism, anxiety, and the list continues. While the situation in Psalm 108 is not explicitly stated, it appears David is facing an upcoming battle. Psalm 108 is unique because it is composed of words from Psalm 57:7–11 and Psalm 60:5–12. These psalms reveal how David was experiencing persecution and defeat. In light of this, David prays to the Lord and asks Him for victory. In the battles of our lives, Psalm 108 gives us this resounding hope—victory belongs to the Lord.

David begins by stating that his heart is confident. Yet this confidence does not come from himself. David's confidence is in the Lord, and he praises God in response. In verse 2, David uses the harp and lyre in his worship for the Lord. David also says he will wake up the dawn, most likely using his instruments of praise. His praise also goes public in verse 3 as David says he will praise God among the people and nations. For David to praise God among the people and nations most likely meant he was praising the Lord among those against him. Nevertheless, David is adamant about rejoicing in the Lord for all to hear. Even in a time of fear, David's zeal for worship encourages us to worship the Lord in every season. In seasons of the unknown, we should never stop praising. Even if we do not know what is ahead, our hearts can be confident in the Lord. Like David, our public praise is an opportunity for others to hear the greatness of God. Praising God publicly in hard times is a powerful gospel witness.

We see David's reasons for praise in verses 4-5 as he describes the character of God. David writes how God's faithfulness extends high above the heavens. He also praises God for being exalted in the heavens, alluding to God's transcendence and sovereignty. David's heart is confident because of who God is. Because God is faithful and sovereign, He is sure God will help him in his time of need. We, too, should have confidence because of who God is. In the face of the unknown, we can find peace knowing God is faithfully caring for and protecting us. We can confidently move forward as God sovereignly guides our steps.

After these praises, David asks for God's help. David prays for God to save and answer him, so David and his army can be rescued. Verse 7 can also be translated to say, "God has promised by his holiness" (ESV). By promising according to His nature, God declares His trustworthiness. God can never lie, so whatever He promises will always come to pass. In verses 7-9, God declares control and victory over areas of the Promised Land. David can confidently trust in the faithfulness of the Lord. God has promised to help him, and God will see this promise through.

Yet David seems anxious about God's help in verses 10-11. He writes how he does not know who will lead him and how it feels as if God has rejected him and his army. He prays again for God's help against his enemies, knowing human help pales in comparison to help from the Lord (verses 12-13). David knows He needs God to secure the victory. This is why, in verse 13, he says, "With God we will perform valiantly." David recognizes he will not be successful without the Lord's help. Victory lies in the hands of the Lord. There is nothing we can do in our own strength to overcome the battles we face.

David's phrase, "With God we will perform valiantly," is a phrase we can adapt to our current circumstances. Amid suffering, fear of the future, or seasons of questioning, we can confidently say, "the Lord will perform valiantly!" Yet victory in the Lord does not mean we will always receive what we want. Our idea of victory and what God sees as victory can sometimes differ. Even still, His promise of victory means we can press on and through anything we may face.

Paul writes in Philippians 4:13 how he can do all things through Christ's strength. Like David, Paul knew victory was found in the Lord, and even if he walked through difficult situations, he would find rest in the strength and help of Christ.

As followers of Jesus, we have victory in Christ. In Romans 8:31-32, Paul writes, "What then are we to say about these things? If God is for us, who is against us? He did not even spare his own Son but offered him up for us all. How will he not also with him grant us everything?" Christ's triumph over sin and death gives us victory over sin. His defeat declares us free from the bondage of sin forever. Therefore, our confidence is rooted in the victory of Christ. As believers, we can walk through anything in this life knowing we have victory. We can rejoice that God's help and strength will help us fight battles of sin and fear. Even if suffering persists, we can find rest in Christ's future victory. Knowing the battle has been won gives us the confidence to fight our battles on this side of eternity. We do not fight against sin hopelessly but triumphantly. Forevermore, we have a God who is victorious.

EVEN IF SUFFERING PERSISTS, we can find rest in Christ's future victory.

WHAT SITUATION ARE YOU IN RIGHT NOW IN WHICH YOU
CAN RESPOND, "GOD WILL PERFORM VALIANTLY"?

_____

HOW DOES THIS PSALM ENCOURAGE YOU WHEN YOU FEAR THE UNKNOWN?

_____

WHY IS IT IMPORTANT TO RECOGNIZE THAT OUR VICTORY COMES FROM THE LORD?

_____

At some point, most of us have likely had someone against us. Maybe that person spread lies and gossiped about us, or maybe a person we thought was a friend betrayed us. In Psalm 109, David prays against an enemy who has slandered him. In response, David prays for God to bring about justice through judgment. Through this psalm, David demonstrates what our response as believers should be when injustice occurs to us.

Psalm 109 is an Imprecatory Psalm. This type of psalm involves invoking judgment or curses upon an enemy. The language used in Imprecatory Psalms can seem alarming because of its violent or cruel words. Because of this, it is important to have the correct perspective when approaching this type of psalm. These psalms should be seen as for our instruction, not for our imitation. While strong in language, these psalms offer principles we can apply to our personal prayer lives. It is good and right to pray that God would bring justice, but how we pray for justice matters. Both love for others and hatred of evil should be kept in balance with the help of the Holy Spirit. We can pray for justice while following Jesus's teaching to pray for and love our enemies (Matthew 5:44).

David starts this psalm first and foremost with praise (verse 1). He comes before the God he praises to pray and lament over the actions of others. We learn how David's character is being attacked as his enemies spread lies and slander him (verse 2). Even worse, they have rejected the love and good David has shown them (verse 4). Yet, David continues to pray to God for His help (verses 4-5). This reminds us to keep praying when we face rejection in our own lives. Rejection from others propels us to come before the God who will never reject us.

In verses 6-20, David expresses prayers of judgment over his enemies. While David wants to see justice occur, we see from his prayers no attempt to take justice into his own hands. He asks God to be the One to bring about justice instead of seeking personal retaliation. This teaches us we can leave matters of injustice in God's hands. We can find peace when we or others are wronged, knowing God will enact justice, either now or in the future. In doing so, we reflect Jesus, who did not retaliate when He experienced injustice. 1 Peter 2:23 tells us when Jesus was insulted, he did not retaliate but "entrusted himself to the one who judges justly." We follow Jesus's example by entrusting ourselves to God, who is our just judge. We can leave vengeance in His hands, knowing God will bring restoration from all acts of injustice.

In verse 16, we learn the reason for David's prayers for judgment. His enemy failed to show kindness to others but persecuted the suffering, needy, and brokenhearted. This person dishonored people, which means he dishonored God. Sin against others should be taken seriously This challenges us not to turn a blind eye to sins of injustice. As believers, we should be mindful of what occurs around us and pray fervently for God to bring justice to those who are oppressed or wronged.

Yet David does not remain focused on his enemy but shifts his mind to the Lord. David asks for God's help in his current suffering. He is honest with God about the affliction his enemies have brought upon him. In verse 26, David asks God to help him and save him according to God's faithful love. David asks God to help him as a testimony of God's power and glory. He writes in verse 27 how he wants God's help, so others will see it is God who delivered and rescued him. Even in a painful situation, David wants God to be glorified. This encourages us to use our own experiences of restoration as opportunities to point to God's grace and glory. When God helps or delivers us from affliction, we can joyfully say to others, "This is God's doing!"

Just as David starts this psalm with praise, he ends this psalm with praise (verses 30-31). Because of God's faithfulness, David will thank the Lord and praise Him in public. Ultimately, he praises God for how He shows His faithful love to His people. In verse 31, David writes how God stands at the right hands of the needy, ready to save them. This is a sweet picture for us to consider in our daily lives. God does not stand at a distance from His people. He is always by our side, ready to help and strengthen us through anything we face. Our hope in times of suffering is that we have a great deliverer on our side.

In our own experiences of rejection and persecution, we should remember how Jesus was rejected and persecuted for our sake. Jesus knows what it is like for people to slander Him, betray Him, and harm Him. The enemy in this passage deserves punishment for his sin, but we, too, deserve punishment for the sin we have committed against God. Before Christ, we were enemies of God, yet Jesus loved us by dying for us. His exhortation to love our enemies should cut us to our heart, knowing we, too, were once enemies of God. The grace we have received from Christ should be a grace we want our enemies to experience.

Jesus modeled prayer for enemies while on the cross by asking God to forgive those persecuting Him (Luke 23:34). In our own prayer lives, we should follow Jesus's example by praying for our enemies. We should pray that these people will be moved to repentance and come to know the Lord. God is a God of deliverance and restoration who can turn even the most wayward heart toward Him.

God is a God of deliverance and restoration WHO CAN TURN EVEN THE MOST WAYWARD HEART TOWARD HIM.

WHY IS IT HARD TO LEAVE JUSTICE IN GOD'S HANDS? HOW DOES THIS PASSAGE
CHALLENGE YOU TO REFRAIN FROM PERSONAL RETALIATION?

HOW DOES THIS PSALM ENCOURAGE YOU TO PRAY
IN TIMES OF REJECTION OR PERSECUTION?

HOW CAN YOU PRAY FOR YOUR ENEMIES WITHOUT WISHING HARM AGAINST THEM?
WHAT DOES IT LOOK LIKE TO EXTEND LOVE AND GRACE TOWARD THEM AS JESUS DID?

Psalm 110 is a unique psalm because it is a prophecy from David. Scholars believe God allowed David to see a vision of Him speaking to another, and this is David's recording of that experience. As the most quoted psalm in the New Testament, these words are central to understanding Jesus Christ. In fact, the other "Lord" this psalm refers to is Jesus. Through the power of the Holy Spirit, David penned this psalm, prophesying about the coming Messiah, whose rule and reign are worthy to be praised.

The psalm can be divided into three sections, each declaring a title of Jesus: King, Priest, and Warrior. In verses 1-3, Jesus is described as King. Verse 1 describes how David witnesses the Lord speaking to His Lord. For David to record the words, "the Lord to my Lord" communicates equality between these two beings. David does not see a difference in power between God and Jesus. God's command for Jesus to sit at His right hand also demonstrates Jesus's equality with the Father. Throughout Scripture, Jesus is described as being at the right hand of the Father, indicating their equal rule and reign (Colossians 3:1). David writes in verse 3 how Jesus's people will volunteer on His day of battle, consecrating themselves to be in holy splendor. This verse describes the joyful desire of believers to serve and obey Jesus. By using the word "volunteers," David indicates a willing servitude. As believers, it is our joy, not an obligation, to serve Jesus. In response to what He has done for us on the cross, we delight to obey Him and grow in Christlikeness to glorify Him. As King, Jesus deserves worship. As we read of His exalted state in these verses, we should be moved to glorify Him.

Next, David describes Jesus as a priest. God's words in verse 4 form a solemn oath. For God to make an oath He will never take back demonstrates His complete trustworthiness. What is His oath? It is a promise that Jesus is a priest forever, "according to the pattern of Melchizedek" (verse 4). For some of us, Melchizedek may sound like a strange and unfamiliar name. But this name points us back to Genesis 14:18-20 where Melchizedek is described as both a priest and a king. Typically, the office of priest and king were separate in the Old Testament. Yet God declares that, following the pattern of Melchizedek, Jesus is a priest and a king. However, unlike Melchizedek, Jesus remains our Priest-King forever.

The author of Hebrews quotes verse 4 in Hebrews 7 to describe Jesus as the Great High Priest. He writes in verses 24-25, "But because he remains forever, he holds his priesthood permanently. Therefore, he is able to save completely those who come to God through him, since he always lives to intercede for them." As our Great High Priest, Jesus intercedes on behalf of believers. In the Old Testament, the priest's job was to make sacrifices on behalf of the people to atone for their sins. Jesus gave Himself as a sacrifice by dying on the cross on behalf of all mankind. He intercedes for us by providing atonement for our sins, forgiving our sins, and restoring us to God.

Because Jesus is at the right hand of the Father, He continues to intercede for us (Romans 8:34). This means when we sin, Jesus is our advocate who pleads our innocence before God. We remain guiltless forever because of our Great High Priest. In response to our Great High Priest, we should be full of gratitude. As sinners, we do not deserve Jesus's sacrifice, yet He died on the cross for our sake. His desire to continue to intercede for us demonstrates His great love and grace. Every day, we should thank Jesus for being our Priest-King. He is not only over all things, but He has come near to make us new.

Finally, Verses 5-7 describe Jesus as a Warrior. In verse 1, God tells Jesus to sit at His right hand until He makes enemies His footstool. In verses 5-7, we see this promise come to fruition. Revelation 19 fulfills these verses as Jesus is described as a great warrior bringing judgment upon unrepentant sinners. The language in verses 5-7 may alarm us, but it speaks to the reality of punishment sin deserves. For those of us in Christ, we are rescued from this judgment. But the reality of this punishment for sinners apart from Christ should encourage us to share the gospel. As we desire for sinners to be saved from this judgment, we realize we have an active role to play in evangelism. In light of this day, we look forward with hope as Christ's deliverance will rid the world of sin forever.

David's prophecy causes us to marvel at Jesus, our King, Priest, and Warrior. While David looked ahead to the Messiah, for us today, the Messiah has already come. As followers of Christ, we are in an intimate relationship with our Priest-King. Every day, we receive the blessings of Jesus's lordship and priesthood. In response, may we joyfully obey and serve the One who brought us into His kingdom through His sacrifice, the One who cleansed us from sin and made us new, the One who actively fights for us and with us. Praise be to our great Priest, King, and Warrior!

Every day, we receive the blessings
OF JESUS'S LORDSHIP AND PRIESTHOOD.

READ HEBREWS 9:11-14. ACCORDING TO THESE VERSES, WHAT HAS
CHRIST DONE FOR US AS OUR HIGH PRIEST?

_____

HOW DOES JESUS'S INTERCESSION COMFORT YOU WHEN YOU SIN?

_____

WHY IS IT IMPORTANT TO SEE JESUS AS KING? HOW CAN
YOU DAILY SUBMIT TO HIM AS KING?

_____

Scripture Memory

I WILL FERVENTLY THANK THE LORD WITH MY MOUTH; I WILL PRAISE HIM IN THE PRESENCE OF MANY. FOR HE STANDS AT THE RIGHT HAND OF THE NEEDY TO SAVE HIM FROM THOSE WHO WOULD CONDEMN HIM.

Psalm 109:30-31

SUMMARIZE THE MAIN POINTS FROM THIS WEEK'S SCRIPTURE READINGS.

WHAT DID YOU OBSERVE FROM THIS WEEK'S PASSAGES ABOUT GOD AND HIS CHARACTER?

WHAT DO THIS WEEK'S PASSAGES REVEAL ABOUT THE CONDITION OF MANKIND AND YOURSELF?

HOW DO THESE PASSAGES POINT TO THE GOSPEL?

HOW SHOULD YOU RESPOND TO THESE PASSAGES? WHAT SPECIFIC
ACTION STEPS CAN YOU TAKE THIS WEEK TO APPLY THEM IN YOUR LIFE?

WRITE A PRAYER IN RESPONSE TO YOUR STUDY OF GOD'S WORD. ADORE GOD FOR WHO HE IS,
CONFESS SINS HE REVEALED IN YOUR OWN LIFE, ASK HIM TO EMPOWER YOU TO WALK IN OBE-
DIENCE, AND PRAY FOR ANYONE WHO COMES TO MIND AS YOU STUDY.

God's Unchangeable Love (Psalm 106)

ISSAC WATTS

God of eternal love,
How fickle are our ways!
And yet how oft did Isr'el prove
Thy constancy of grace!

They saw Thy wonders wrought,
And then Thy praise they sung;
But soon Thy works of power forgot,
And murmured with their tongue.

Now they believe his word
While rocks with rivers flow;
Now with their lusts provoke the Lord,
And he reduced them low.

Yet when they mourned their faults,
He hearkened to their groans,
Brought His own cov'nant to His thoughts,
And called them still His sons.

Their names were in His book,
He saved them from their foes
Oft He chastised, but ne'er forsook
The people that He chose.

Let Isr'el bless the Lord,
Who loved their ancient race
And Christians join the solemn word,
Amen, to all the praise.

Wholehearted Praise

A recurring theme we have seen in our study of the Psalms is the theme of worship. Psalm 111 continues this theme by praising God for all of His wonderful works. All the attention is on the Lord in this psalm, which encourages us to set our gaze on Him alone. The continual exhortation to praise the Lord reminds us how our worship should remain constant. Every day and every moment is an opportunity to praise the Lord.

The psalmist proclaims he will worship the Lord in two different ways in verse 1. The first way is private, as he worships the Lord with all of his heart. The second way is public, as he worships among acquaintances and the congregation. The psalmist's dedication to worship in both of these spheres reminds us that private and public worship are necessary to our spiritual growth. Private worship allows us to take opportunities in our homes and day-to-day lives to praise the Lord individually. Public worship allows us to join with other believers to praise the Lord corporally. The more we worship in both spheres, the more we will see our desires and affections shaped to love and serve the Lord.

In verses 2-4, the psalmist praises three different kinds of works from the Lord: God's creative works, providential works, and redemptive works. The first is God's creative works. In verse 2, the psalmist writes how God's creative acts are "great, studied by all who delight in them." God has given us His creation as a way for us to know Him; Bible scholars and theologians refer to this as general revelation. As we gaze at creation, we marvel at the creative works of God's hands. Yet, our study of creation is meant to point us to the One who created it. Delight in creation causes us to delight in the Creator.

In verse 3, the psalmist speaks to God's providential works. He writes how all God does is "splendid and majestic" and how "his righteousness endures forever." God's providential works are splendid and majestic because God's providence is both mysterious and glorious. It can be hard for us to wrap our minds around how God orchestrates all things according to His will, but this should also lead us to revel in His divine wisdom. From the beginning of time, God's providential hand has worked to accomplish His sovereign will, and that is a reason to rejoice.

Lastly, in verse 4, the psalmist speaks of God's redemptive works. He writes how God is gracious and compassionate, revealing how His redemptive works stem from His character. The psalmist also writes how God causes His redemptive works to be remembered. For the people of Israel, God's redemptive work through the exodus was an impactful event they regularly remembered. For believers today, remembering what Christ has done for us should be a regular rhythm in our lives. God has shown His grace and compassion toward us through Christ's redemptive work on the cross. Gathering together to partake in the Lord's Supper is a special way we collectively remember and meditate on Christ's sacrifice and forgiveness. Yet every day is a day to remember and rejoice over the gospel.

The psalmist continues by listing specific acts of the Lord in verses 5-9. In verse 5, the psalmist writes how God provides for His people. Most likely, the psalmist has in mind the provision of manna that God gave Israel in the wilderness. God is our great provider who graciously meets our daily needs. God's constant provision coincides with how He remembers His covenant forever. Even when Israel was undeserving, God continued to provide for His covenant people. In verse 6, the psalmist speaks to how God showed His power through giving Israel an inheritance. Here, the psalmist is likely referring to the Promised Land. His covenant to Israel involved the gift of the Promised Land, and He was faithful to fulfill this promise. As believers, we have seen God's power through Christ's death and resurrection. By triumphing over sin and death, we see God's power at work. Like the Israelites, believers are given an inheritance of the ultimate Promised Land—eternity in heaven.

The psalmist pauses his list of God's works in verse 7 to proclaim how God's works and His Word are trustworthy. Because God is Holy, all of His acts are just and true. Not one of His acts is executed unfairly or unrighteously. Therefore, we can trust His acts and His Word. The holiness of God encourages us to follow His commands. We know what He says in His Word can be obeyed because of who He is. As we follow and obey His truth, we will reflect the holiness of our God. The truth and uprightness of God's Word mold us into people of truth and uprightness.

In verse 9, the psalmist speaks again to the redemption God has sent His people. Ultimately, God has sent this redemption through Jesus Christ. He has not only ordained His covenant but fulfilled His covenant through the person of Jesus. All of these works of the Lord lead us to the response in verse 10: fear of the Lord. As believers, we are to grow in wisdom by fearing the Lord. To fear the Lord does not mean we become frightened or afraid; it means we revel and delight in who God is. If we want to grow in our fear of the Lord, we must delight in the gospel. The more we remember, reflect, and rejoice in the gospel, the more we will grow in our worship of the Lord. This involves regularly coming to God's Word, listening to and obeying His instructions. God is our Creator, Redeemer, and Provider. May our fear of Him increase as we remember and rejoice in what He has done.

The more we remember, reflect, and rejoice in the gospel, THE MORE WE WILL GROW IN OUR WORSHIP OF THE LORD.

TAKE SOME TIME TO THINK OF SOME EXAMPLES OF GOD'S CREATIVE, PROVIDENTIAL,
AND REDEMPTIVE WORKS, AND LIST THEM IN THE TABLE BELOW.
THESE CAN BE EXAMPLES FROM SCRIPTURE OR YOUR PERSONAL LIFE.

CREATIVE WORKS	PROVIDENTIAL WORKS	REDEMPTIVE WORKS

HOW DOES REGULARLY REMEMBERING AND REJOICING
IN GOD'S WORKS INCREASE OUR FEAR OF HIM?

WHAT ARE SOME WAYS YOU CAN BE MORE INTENTIONAL ABOUT REMEMBERING,
REFLECTING, AND REJOICING IN THE GOSPEL IN YOUR DAILY LIFE?

Full of Delight

READ PSALM 112

Psalm 111 and Psalm 112 are often seen as companions. While Psalm 111 speaks to delighting in God's works, Psalm 112 speaks to delighting in God's Word. God is the main focus in Psalm 111, whereas godliness is the main focus in Psalm 112. Looking at both of these psalms together, we see how God's works lead us to study His Word. By studying His Word, we grow in our fear of the Lord, and in turn, we grow in godliness. By delighting in the Lord and His Word, we become more like the One in whom we delight.

The psalmist picks up where he left off in Psalm 112 by writing how the one who fears the Lord is a happy man. True joy is found by delighting in God's commands. All of what follows in this psalm is connected to the first verse. Godly character and blessing come from obedience to God and His Word.

In verses 2-5, the psalmist speaks to the physical blessing of the godly. The psalmist writes in verse 2 how the godly man will produce a strong and blessed generation. Here, we learn how godliness impacts the children we raise. While it is not promised that our children will come to know the Lord, what a blessing our instruction is to them as we raise them to know and love the Lord. Many of us have seen the fruit of being raised by godly parents in our own lives. Likewise, our godly character shapes the generation that comes after us. May this be an encouragement for parents to see their parenting as impactful.

In verse 3, the psalmist speaks to how the godly receive wealth and riches. We should be careful not to read this verse as promoting the prosperity gospel. God does bless us financially, but He does not promise that following Him will make us wealthy. However, He does promise daily provision for our needs. Our needs are not only met, but as believers, we are certainly "rich" in Christ. While we may not always have physical riches, we will always have spiritual riches through Christ. These include the blessing of a future inheritance, the forgiveness of our sins, and sanctification through the Spirit.

We read in verse 4 how times of suffering and adversity are inevitable for the godly. As believers, we will experience times of darkness, such as physical suffering or the loss of a loved one. Yet what gives us comfort is that "light shines in the darkness for the upright" (verse 4). Jesus is our light in the darkness—He is our hope. John 1:4-5 describes Jesus as having life that is the light of men; this light shines in the darkness, and darkness cannot overcome it. Through Jesus's sacrifice on the cross, we have been given new life that rescues us from the darkness of sin. The light of the gospel cannot be extinguished in times of dark suffering. Even in the moments we walk through the darkness, we have the sure hope that God will help us through.

The psalmist describes the godly person as a generous person in verse 5. The provision given in verse 3 is not to be kept for ourselves but freely given. As believers, we use the blessing we receive in Christ to bless others. We lend generously and give freely to the poor. We also act justly in our business affairs with others. Generosity reflects the gospel. Jesus freely gave up Himself so that we could receive the gift of salvation. Giving to others reflects the grace of the Giver.

In verses 6-8, the psalmist speaks to the emotional blessing of the godly. He writes how the godly will "never be shaken" and "will not fear." As believers, we will sometimes find ourselves in situations that will cause us to feel shaken and fearful, yet we do not have to succumb to fear. The psalmist teaches us the godly are secure and at peace because they trust in the Lord. The more we trust in the Lord, the more our hearts will be assured. It is when we distrust the Lord and His Word that we become easily shaken in trying times. Our hearts are assured when we trust the character of the Lord. Knowing God is faithful helps us trust in Him in times of fear and the unknown. Ultimately, our hearts can be assured because we know what our future holds.

Knowing that God will one day make all things new helps us to stay at peace in our current situations. Even if we walk through hard times, we can be cheered knowing this is not the end. In light of eternity, we can walk through anything.

The psalmist briefly compares and contrasts the ungodly and the godly in verse 10. The ungodly see the blessing of the godly and respond with scorn. Without the Lord, the desires of sinful flesh lead to quite the opposite of the godly life. The godly life is eternal and full of joy, but the ungodly life is transient and full of bitterness. As believers, we should pray eagerly for the ungodly to come to know the Lord. It is a great joy to receive these blessings from our relationship with the Lord, but we should want the same blessings for those who do not know Christ.

The godly life portrayed in these verses should encourage us to continue to grow in godliness. But may we not forget that we grow in godliness by delighting in God's commands, not by trusting in our efforts. The fear of the Lord shapes our lives, so let us daily delight in Him.

The fear of the Lord shapes our lives,
SO LET US DAILY DELIGHT IN HIM.

VERSE 4 TELLS US HOW THE GODLY PERSON IS GRACIOUS, COMPASSIONATE, AND RIGHTEOUS. HOW DOES STUDYING GOD'S WORD FORM US INTO GRACIOUS, COMPASSIONATE, AND RIGHTEOUS PEOPLE?

———————————————

WHAT CHARACTERISTIC OF THE LORD OR TRUTH FROM GOD'S WORD CAN ASSURE YOUR HEART IN TIMES OF FEAR?

———————————————

HOW DOES GENEROSITY AFFECT OUR GOSPEL WITNESS? IN WHAT WAYS CAN YOU BE GENEROUS TO OTHERS THIS WEEK?

———————————————

Who is Like the Lord Our God?

Psalm 113 begins a series of psalms used at Passover. This psalm, in particular, is known as the Egyptian Hallel. "Hallel" means "praise," and we can see why this psalm was titled this way by the language used in the first several verses. The words "praise" or "praised" are used three times in the first three verses. This emphasis on praise may seem repetitive to us, but that is the point! The psalmist's continual reminder to praise God seeks to engrain this rhythm into our lives. The more we do something, the more it becomes habitual. Yet worship is not meant to be a mundane habit; it is a way of life. From the rising sun to the setting sun, we are to praise the Lord (verse 3).

Even though we do not necessarily need a reason to praise God, the psalmist gives us a "why" behind his exhortations in verses 4-9. He begins in verses 4-6 by emphasizing the holiness and transcendence of God. He writes how God is exalted on high, and His exalted position signifies His holiness. God is distinct and set apart. This is why the psalmist says in verse 5, "Who is like the Lord our God?" The answer to this question is "no one"! When we realize no one compares to God, we revel in His holiness. Yet, sometimes, we downplay God's holiness, treating Him as if He is on the same level as earthly things. If we want to remain worshipful in our everyday lives, we must continue to see God as distinct from all He has created. He deserves honor and praise for His great holiness. The psalmist describes God's exalted position in verse 6 by writing how God has to stoop low to observe the heavens and the earth. God's holiness creates distance between Him and His creation.

However, God does not remain distant from His creation. He delights in becoming low for the lowly. In verses 7-9, the psalmist writes of God's active hand among His creation. Hannah quotes these verses in her prayer in 1 Samuel 2:8. In this prayer, Hannah rejoices over how God rescued her from her low state by blessing her with the gift of a child. Mary repeats similar words in her prayer in Luke 1:46-48 after receiving the news of her immaculate conception. She says, "My soul praises the greatness of the Lord, and my spirit rejoices in God my Savior, because he has looked with favor on the humble condition of his servant." God delights in exalting the lowly. He does not stoop low to observe the earth so that He can merely watch the lowly suffer. He raises and lifts up the poor, exalting them to a position with the nobles. Throughout Scripture, we see how God comes to raise up broken people and bless them with His grace.

Yet God took one step further in meeting the lowly by becoming lowly Himself. Jesus left His exalted position to come to earth as a man. He temporarily set aside His glory so that He could be a servant, coming near to heal and save the lowly from their sins. The words we find in verses 7-9 can also describe our relationship with Christ. Because of Christ's sacrifice on the cross, we have been brought out of the trash heap of our sin. Just like Jesus was brought low in His crucifixion and made high after His resurrection, so has our salvation taken us from our low state. Ephesians 2:4-6 tells us, "But God, who is rich in mercy, because of his great love that he had for us, made us alive with Christ even though we were dead in trespasses. You are saved by grace! He also raised us up with him and seated us with him in the heavens in Christ Jesus."

The salvation we have received from Christ should make us proclaim, "Who is like the Lord our God" (verse 5). No other religion centers on a God who made Himself lowly to save His people. We serve the one true God who is holy yet humble, set apart yet near. How could we not give praise to the One who has raised us to a new life in Him? May we wake up every morning with the reminder of our salvation fresh in our minds. May we sing of our salvation as the day passes. May we end our evening with words of praise. Our God is worthy to be praised. Hallelujah!

MAY WE WAKE UP EVERY
MORNING WITH THE REMINDER
OF OUR SALVATION
fresh in our minds.

READ ISAIAH 57:15. WHAT DOES THIS VERSE TEACH US ABOUT GOD?

_____

HOW DOES KNOWING THAT GOD DOES NOT REMAIN AT A DISTANCE ENCOURAGE YOU?
HOW DOES THIS TRUTH HELP YOU IN TIMES OF FEAR OR SUFFERING?

_____

WHAT DOES IT LOOK LIKE TO HAVE A RHYTHM OF DAILY WORSHIP?
HOW CAN YOU IMPLEMENT THIS RHYTHM INTO YOUR LIFE?

_____

Rejoice and Tremble

God is a God of redemption. From the beginning of the Bible to the end, we see God committed to saving and redeeming His people. Psalm 114 continues the Passover Psalms by rejoicing over God's acts of redemption. God declared His redemption to Israel through the exodus, but He did not stop redeeming His people there. Through Psalm 114, the psalmist praises God for the other great acts of redemption He has shown Israel.

The psalmist begins by writing about how Israel became God's sanctuary and dominion after the exodus (verses 1-2). God's plan of deliverance for Israel involved forming them into a people for His namesake. God chose Israel to be a holy and set-apart nation with the purpose of giving Him glory. Throughout Israel's history, God continued to show the Israelites they belonged to Him by His covenantal faithfulness. The exodus was certainly not Israel's only act of deliverance from God, for God delivered Israel time and time again.

Verses 3-8 speak to specific events of God's deliverance. Verse 3 describes the waters of the Red Sea and the Jordan River. During Israel's flee from Egypt, God caused the waters of the Red Sea to part, so they could escape on dry land (Exodus 14:15-29). Later, when Israel was journeying into the Promised Land, they needed to cross the raging Jordan River. Like the Red Sea, God parted the waters of the Jordan River, and the Israelites crossed safely (Joshua 3). The psalmist personifies the waters of the Red Sea and the Jordan River by writing they "turned back" and "fled." What caused them to turn back and flee? It was God's power alone.

Verse 4 describes the powerful experience of God coming down upon Mount Sinai. This was a pivotal event in Israel's history because it was here that God gave Moses the Ten Commandments. God's powerful presence descending on Mount Sinai caused the mountains and hills to move like "skipping rams and lambs" (Psalm 114:6). This is detailed in Exodus 19:16, where the arrival of God's presence is described as "thunder and lightning, a thick cloud on the mountain, and a very loud trumpet sound, so that all the people in the camp shuddered." Meanwhile, Verse 8 describes the Israelites' experience in the wilderness. They were thirsty and asked Moses to give them something to drink. God instructed Moses to strike a nearby rock. When he did, water flowed for the people to drink (Exodus 17:1-6).

These acts of God's deliverance describe God's power in three ways. First, we see God's power over creation. The sea, river, and mountains all moved because of God's control over them. God has power over all He has created. Second, we see God's power to save. The events at the Red Sea and the Jordan River show God's desire to redeem His people. He did not want His people to remain in danger, so He rescued them. Lastly, we find God's power to provide. His provision of water in the wilderness describes His care for His people. God provides for the needs of His people and delights in taking care of them.

These three aspects of God's power are still relevant to our lives today. God's control over all of creation should give us comfort in troubling times. Because nothing is out of God's control, we can trust Him. God's power to provide also encourages us to trust Him. Knowing God provides for our needs encourages us to have faith in times of fear or the unknown. God is powerful over even the most trying circumstances.

Ultimately, however, God has shown us His power to save through His Son. Christ's work on the cross is His most powerful work of deliverance. In fact, God's acts of redemption in the Old Testament point to Christ's future act of redemption in the New Testament. Colossians 1:13-14 tells us God has "rescued us from the domain of darkness and transferred us into the kingdom of the Son he loves. In him we have redemption, the forgiveness of sins." God has delivered us from sin and brought us into His family. The same power that caused the sea and rivers to part, the mountains to quake, and the rocks to burst forth is the same power that raised Jesus from the grave. What's more, this same power lives in us as believers (Romans 8:11).

These experiences in Israel's history cause the psalmist to taunt nature in verses 5-6. He uses rhetorical questions to drive home his point: it was God who caused them to move. But the psalmist does not speak only to these elements of creation but to all of creation in verse 7. He commands the whole earth to tremble at the presence of God. For Israel to be obedient to God, they, too, needed to tremble in reverent fear. This command to "tremble" does not mean we are to be afraid of God but in awe of His mighty hand. While God never needs to prove Himself, part of the reason He performed these great acts was to show the Israelites who He was. For Israel to worship Him alone, they needed to see that God was bigger than anything else. For Israel to serve and obey Him, they needed a sense of awe over His power. In the same way, we need to be in awe of our great God daily.

Just as the Israelites remembered God's works of deliverance, we, too, must remember Christ's work of deliverance. God's powerful work of redemption in our lives should cause us to tremble—not in fear but in delight! We are in an intimate relationship with an all-powerful God who loves us and has brought us to Himself.

God's powerful work of redemption in our lives SHOULD CAUSE US TO TREMBLE——NOT IN FEAR BUT IN DELIGHT!

WHAT DOES IT LOOK LIKE PRACTICALLY TO "TREMBLE" IN FRONT OF THE LORD?

HOW DOES GOD'S POWER ENCOURAGE OUR OBEDIENCE TO AND WORSHIP OF HIM?

OF THE THREE ASPECTS OF GOD'S POWER (POWER OVER CREATION, POWER TO SAVE, AND POWER TO PROVIDE), WHICH ONE SPEAKS TO YOU MOST IN YOUR CURRENT CIRCUMSTANCES? WHY?

Not to Us, But to Your Name Give Glory

READ PSALM 115

Our world loves glory. When we turn on the television, we see athletes who thrive on their team winning their game. When we open up social media, we see celebrities post certain photos to win likes. As humans, our sinful nature is prideful. Something about receiving praise and glory satisfies us. And if we are not careful, we can chase after it ruthlessly. But the words of Psalm 115 open up with a message quite different from what the world teaches us.

The psalmist prays in verse 1 for God to receive the glory—not man. This is a prayer of humility. How often do we pray this way? Even if we are in Christ, we can still struggle for praise and glory. But the psalmist reminds us whose glory matters the most. We live for God's glory and not our own. In the moments we find ourselves struggling with a yearning for affirmation, may verse 1 be our prayer. Praying this truth regularly will humble our hearts and cause us to seek God's glory first.

In verse 2, the psalmist writes of the nations' reaction toward God's people. They taunt God's people and mock His power. Yet, the psalmist does not respond with ridicule but words of truth. He speaks to God's sovereignty in verse 3, proclaiming God is exalted on high and does what He so wills. Even if others mock God or mock us for believing in God, we know who God is. We trust God is ruling and working, even if others do not recognize or believe in Him.

Ultimately, we trust God because He is worthy to be worshiped. In verses 4-8, the psalmist exposes the futility of idols. With each one of the verses, we can see how God is greater than any idols. Verse 4 says idols are crafted by human hands, but God is self-existent. He is made by no one. Verse 5 says idols cannot speak, but from the beginning of Scripture, we see a God who speaks to His creation. Verse 5 also says idols cannot see, but God sees everything. Verse 6 says idols cannot hear, but God listens to His creation. Verse 7 says idols cannot move or touch, but God is active within His creation. Not only this, but through Jesus's incarnation, God has touched His creation. Unlike idols, God has an intimate relationship with His creation.

Verse 8 reveals the sad reality of those who worship and trust in idols: they become like them. We become what we behold. When we worship idols, we keep ourselves from being shaped into the people we were created to be. When we worship idols such as perfectionism and materialism, we become prideful and selfish. However, worship to God grows us to be more like God. He is who we are to worship so we can grow in godliness and Christlikeness. These verses should cause us to examine our worship. Who or what are you allowing to shape you?

When we see God's ultimate glory compared to idols, we recognize God alone is to be worshiped. We do not need created objects of worship for life and satisfaction. We need the Creator. In response, let us think critically about the things in which we place our trust apart from God. Let us make efforts to either remove them or seek God before them.

In verses 9-13, the psalmist calls for all of Israel to trust the Lord. He starts broadly with the nation of Israel as a whole and moves down to individuals who fear the Lord. He exhorts them to trust the Lord, for God is "their help and shield" (Psalm 115:9-11). The psalmist also writes how the Lord will bless all of Israel, from the smallest to the greatest. This reveals how God blesses all those who fear Him and not just those who are in high positions. All of God's people are blessed.

The theme of blessing continues in verse 14 as the psalmist prays God will bless Israel by causing their nation to be fruitful. He also prays for God's general blessing over Israel in verse 15. Yet, in the verses that follow, we see that God's blessing encourages us to bless Him. Following the prayer from verse 1, we respond in praise to God over His good gifts. Whatever prosperity we have in our life is due to the Lord. Therefore, we lift our hands and give Him the glory. As God's people, we are to bless Him forever.

The psalmist writes in verses 17-18 how the dead do not and cannot praise the Lord. But as God's people, we are alive. We are alive because Christ has made us so. Through His death and resurrection, Jesus has made those who were once dead come alive (Ephesians 2: 4-5). As people who have been brought from death to life, we praise the One who has made us alive. When tempted to live for our glory, we must remember what Jesus has done for us. Continually reminding ourselves of the gospel humbles our hearts. Jesus deserves the glory for our salvation. He deserves praise for giving us new life. May the good news of the gospel lift our voices in worship. Every day, let us say, "Not to us, Lord, not to us, but to your name give glory because of your faithful love, because of your truth" (Psalm 115:1).

MAY THE GOOD NEWS OF THE GOSPEL
lift our voices in worship.

HOW ARE YOU TEMPTED TO SEEK AFTER YOUR OWN GLORY? WHAT DOES IT LOOK
LIKE PRACTICALLY TO LIVE FOR GOD'S GLORY INSTEAD OF YOUR OWN?

HOW DO THE IDOLS WE WORSHIP FAIL TO GIVE US ONLY WHAT GOD CAN GIVE US?
WHAT IDOL(S) ARE YOU WORSHIPING NOW THAT YOU NEED TO LAY DOWN?

IN WHAT WAYS HAVE YOU SEEN THE LORD BLESS YOU? SPEND SOME TIME
IN PRAYER THANKING THE LORD FOR HOW HE HAS BLESSED YOU.

Scripture Memory

THE FEAR OF THE LORD IS THE BEGINNING
OF WISDOM; ALL WHO FOLLOW HIS
INSTRUCTIONS HAVE GOOD INSIGHT.
HIS PRAISE ENDURES FOREVER.

Psalm 111:10

Week Five Reflection

SUMMARIZE THE MAIN POINTS FROM THIS WEEK'S SCRIPTURE READINGS.

WHAT DID YOU OBSERVE FROM THIS WEEK'S PASSAGES ABOUT GOD AND HIS CHARACTER?

WHAT DO THIS WEEK'S PASSAGES REVEAL ABOUT THE CONDITION OF MANKIND AND YOURSELF?

Read Psalms 111-115

HOW DO THESE PASSAGES POINT TO THE GOSPEL?

HOW SHOULD YOU RESPOND TO THESE PASSAGES? WHAT SPECIFIC
ACTION STEPS CAN YOU TAKE THIS WEEK TO APPLY THEM IN YOUR LIFE?

WRITE A PRAYER IN RESPONSE TO YOUR STUDY OF GOD'S WORD. ADORE GOD FOR WHO HE IS,
CONFESS SINS HE REVEALED IN YOUR OWN LIFE, ASK HIM TO EMPOWER YOU TO WALK IN OBE-
DIENCE, AND PRAY FOR ANYONE WHO COMES TO MIND AS YOU STUDY.

Not to Ourselves, Who are but Dust (Psalm 115)

ISSAC WATTS

Not to ourselves, who are but dust,
Not to ourselves is glory due,
Eternal God, Thou only just,
Thou only gracious, wise, and true.

Shine forth in all Thy dreadful name;
Why should a heathen's haughty tongue
Insult us, and, to raise our shame,
Say, "Where's the God you've served so long?"

The God we serve maintains His throne
Above the clouds, beyond the skies;
Through all the earth His will is done;
He knows our groans, He hears our cries.

But the vain idols they adore
Are senseless shapes of stone and wood;
At best a mass of glitt'ring ore,
A silver saint or golden god.

With eyes and ears they carve their head;
Deaf are their ears, their eyes are blind;
In vain are costly off'rings made,
And vows are scattered in the wind.

Their feet were never made to move,
Nor hands to save when mortals pray;
Mortals that pay them fear or love
Seem to be blind and deaf as they.

O Isr'el! make the Lord thy hope,
Thy help, thy refuge, and thy rest;
The Lord shall build thy ruins up,
And bless the people and the priest.

The dead no more can speak thy praise,
They dwell in silence and the grave;
But we shall live to sing Thy grace,
And tell the world Thy power to save.

Lord, Save Me!

READ PSALM 116

How should we respond as believers in times of suffering? This is the question the psalmist answers in Psalm 116. Titled "Thanks to God for Deliverance," Psalm 116 describes an unknown person's response to God for delivering him from suffering. His words not only remind us how we are not alone in our suffering, but they teach us how to view God in our suffering.

The psalmist opens by revealing how God listens to us in our suffering (verses 1-2). He writes how he loves the Lord because He extends a listening ear. This psalmist does not seem to have a casual attitude toward the listening ear of God. The fact that God listens to him causes him to respond with love. Because the Lord has turned His ear toward him, the psalmist will continue to call out to Him in prayer forever. In times of suffering, do we pray to the Lord? Do we feel as if God listens to us? These verses affirm God does listen to our prayers during suffering. God turns toward us and extends His ear to our cries. Knowing God always hears us should encourage us to pray to Him continuously. God bends His ear to those in pain.

In verses 3-4, the psalmist recounts his plight. While we do not know the details of his suffering, the language of "ropes of death" and "torments of Sheol" indicates personal suffering leading him close to death. Some of us may have experienced a similar situation, whether it be a life-threatening illness or a freak accident. But others may know what it is like to feel as if there are ropes of death entangling us. Many of us have walked through some hard days when it feels like we are in deep darkness. The psalmist teaches us in verse 4 that we are to call out to God in times of suffering. We know from verses 1-2 that God hears our cries, so we too can cry out, "Lord, save me!" when we are facing trouble.

Calling to mind the Lord's character is also important in times of suffering. The psalmist writes how the Lord is gracious, righteous, and compassionate. God has revealed to the psalmist His faithfulness through his deliverance from suffering. Even if the psalmist experiences suffering again, he can remember the gracious, righteous, and compassionate nature of the Lord. It is important for us to remember how we view God in suffering because this determines whether we will trust Him. Knowing God is gracious, righteous, and compassionate encourages us to have hope. The character of God encourages us to cling to Him in suffering and trust that He will help us through.

The psalmist says he is also encouraged to trust the Lord through God's deliverance. He writes in verse 7 how his soul can find rest in God's goodness. Verses 8 reveals how the Lord rescued the psalmist from death, grief, and stumbling. Because of the Lord's deliverance from death, the psalmist can walk in the land of the living (Psalm 116:9). The way the New Testament describes walking in the land of the living is to "walk in the light" (1 John 1:5-7).

Because Christ has rescued us from death, we walk in His marvelous light. Daily, we walk in the light by following the Lord and walking in obedience. Walking in the light also describes a life of joy. If you are on a dark path, you are often fearful and prone to stumbling. But a path full of light fills you with comfort and gives you confident steps. As believers, it is our joy to walk in the light for the rest of our lives.

In verses 10-11, the psalmist writes how he did not lose faith—even in his suffering. Even though he faced oppression, he chose to believe in the Lord. Even though he was afraid, he trusted in the Lord rather than man. In our own moments of suffering, these verses encourage us to have faith in who God is and what He has promised. Our faith can remain strong—even when everything around us is falling apart.

All of what God has done for the psalmist causes him to ask how he can repay the Lord (Psalm 116:12). As believers, we are given the gift of salvation through Christ. We can never repay His grace, but we can respond to His grace. But how? The psalmist gives us the answer in verse 13: we can respond to His grace by receiving the gift of salvation and following the Lord. The cup of salvation in verse 13 contrasts the cup of God's wrath, which is described throughout Scripture as a cup to be poured out over unrepentant sinners (Jeremiah 25:15). Jesus willingly took the cup of wrath on the cross. The wrath of God was poured out upon Him so that we could receive forgiveness. We receive the cup of salvation because Jesus received the cup of wrath.

In response to this great gift of grace, we live lives of gratitude and service to the Lord. The psalmist writes in verses 14-19 how he is God's servant, and as His servant, he will fulfill his vows. In other words, he will be faithful in obedience to the Lord. As followers of Christ, we, too, can say along with the psalmist, "You have loosened my bonds" (Psalm 116:16). Christ's sacrifice on the cross has broken our bondage to sin. We are no longer slaves to sin but joyful servants of Christ (Romans 6:17-18). Daily, we respond to our freedom by faithfully obeying the Lord through the help and power of the Holy Spirit.

How should we respond as believers in times of suffering? Let us respond with trust, hope, and obedience. Although we experience hardship in this life, we have the promise of God's nearness, help, and deliverance. Even in the darkness of suffering, we walk in the light of the Lord.

EVEN IN THE DARKNESS OF SUFFERING,
we walk in the light of the Lord.

HOW DO YOU TYPICALLY RESPOND IN TIMES OF SUFFERING? IN YOUR OWN MOMENTS OF SUFFERING, HOW CAN YOU APPLY WHAT YOU HAVE LEARNED FROM THE PSALMIST'S RESPONSE?

_____

IN PSALM 116, THE PSALMIST CALLS ON THE NAME OF THE LORD FOUR TIMES. WHAT DOES IT LOOK LIKE TO CALL ON THE NAME OF THE LORD IN YOUR TIMES OF SUFFERING?

_____

FROM WHAT TROUBLE OR SORROW HAS GOD DELIVERED YOU? HOW CAN THESE ACTS OF DELIVERANCE GIVE YOU HOPE WHEN YOU ENCOUNTER TROUBLE AND SORROW AGAIN?

_____

All Nations and Peoples

Psalm 117 can be captured by the phrase "short and sweet." If we are not careful, we can skip over this psalm due to its brevity. But the length of this psalm can also cause us to receive the heart of its message immediately. Its emphasis is similar to Psalm 96, calling all nations and peoples to praise God. In just two verses, Psalm 117 packs a punch by drawing us to the deep desire of the Lord—the desire for every tribe and nation to know and worship Him.

Verse 1 calls for all nations and people to glorify and praise the Lord. The psalmist is speaking to people groups all over the world. From the beginning of Scripture, we learn of God's plan to bring people of all nationalities to know Him. In Genesis 12, God spoke to Abraham and told him, "I will make you into a great nation" (Genesis 12:2) and "all the peoples on earth will be blessed through you" (Genesis 12:3). We see this promise come to fruition as God forms the people of Israel into a holy and set-apart nation. Yet, in the New Testament, this promise expands even more as both Jews (Abraham's descendants) and Gentiles (non-Jewish people) are brought into the family of God. The gospel of Jesus was not exclusively for Jews, but it was also an invitation to Gentiles. This was revolutionary as Jews often mistreated Gentiles for not belonging to the line of Israel. God's plan to bring Gentiles into His family reveals how all people are important to God and therefore, should be important to us. The gospel is for every person.

In Romans 15:8-9, Paul writes how Christ's sacrifice on the cross was "to confirm the promises to the fathers, and so that Gentiles may glorify God for his mercy." Later quoting Psalm 117:1, Paul offers an invitation to the Gentiles in Romans 15:10: "Praise the Lord, all you Gentiles; let all the peoples praise him." God desires all nations and peoples to know and worship Him—not just some. We should not see the family of God as including only those who look or sound like us. The throne room of God in Revelation 7 describes people of all tribes, nations, and tongues. This future picture of heaven should animate us to share the gospel with the nations. God's heart for the nations should be our heart.

In verse 2, the psalmist explains why all nations and peoples should praise and glorify God. God's faithful love to us is great, and His faithfulness endures forever. As followers of Christ, we should want others to experience the faithful love of the Lord. Knowing who God is should make us excited to share about Him with others. If God was cold rather than loving, fickle rather than faithful, we would not want to share about Him. But God is a God of everlasting faithfulness whose faithful love toward us is great. How can we not share about this great God? God has declared His faithful love toward us through Christ.

As followers of Jesus, it is our joy to bring this message of salvation to people all over the world.

For us to share with the nations, we need to see the nations as a priority. Some people have not heard the name of Jesus. But there are also people of different cultures and nationalities down the street and in our cities—people who do not know Jesus. This should motivate us to get to know people from other cultures. You can do this by seeing if your local church partners with any cultural ministries in your area. Or you can see if there are opportunities within your local church to serve on a cross-cultural short- or long-term mission trip.

But most importantly, if we want the nations to praise God, we must praise God. We naturally talk about what or who we love. Our love for the Lord should cause us to continually praise and glorify Him. The more we praise and glorify God personally, the more we want to publicly praise and glorify Him. As we publicly praise God, we create opportunities for people to hear the name of Jesus. Seeing our joy can cause others to desire to know more about the God we proclaim.

The brevity of this psalm encourages us to focus on what matters most: the gospel. As followers of Christ, we should take seriously the Great Commission, given to us by Jesus in Matthew 28:18-20. Every day, we should live missionally by looking for opportunities to speak the gospel to those around us. If we want all nations and peoples to praise God, we need to see our role in bringing the gospel to the nations. So, let us go and make His name known.

Every day, we should live missionally
BY LOOKING FOR OPPORTUNITIES
TO SPEAK THE GOSPEL TO
THOSE AROUND US.

READ ROMANS 10:14-15. HOW DO THESE VERSES REVEAL THE IMPORTANCE OF
SHARING THE GOSPEL? HOW DO THESE VERSES ENCOURAGE YOU TO SHARE?

—————————————————

WHY IS IT IMPORTANT THAT GOD WANTS ALL NATIONS AND PEOPLES TO KNOW HIM?
WHAT HAPPENS WHEN GOD'S PEOPLE DO NOT SHARE HIS HEART FOR THE NATIONS?

—————————————————

WHAT ARE SOME PRACTICAL WAYS YOU CAN REACH THE NATIONS WITH THE GOSPEL?

—————————————————

The Lord's Right Hand Performs Valiantly

READ PSALM 118

When Jesus and His disciples gathered for the Last Supper, Psalm 118 is the last psalm they most likely read before Christ's betrayal and arrest. Reading this psalm through the lens of Jesus's experience provides another layer of depth. While this psalm is written from the perspective of an unnamed king, it points us to King Jesus, whose victory on the cross bought our salvation.

The psalmist opens with an exhortation to praise God for His enduring, faithful love. In light of who God is, the psalmist calls all of Israel to joyfully say: "His faithful love endures forever" (Psalm 118:1). While this psalm emphasizes victory, the driving point of its message is God's faithful love. It is because of God's faithful love that believers receive victory.

In verses 5-7, the psalmist gives a personal testimony of God's faithfulness in his life. He writes how in a time of distress, he called out to the Lord. God answered his call and set him in a special place of security. Knowing the faithfulness of the Lord, the psalmist describes how he can confidently say the Lord is for him, and he will not fear. The great protection of the Lord enables him to not fear humans who rise against him. In light of the greatness of God, fear of man subsides. In moments of trouble, we do not need to fear the actions or the words of man. God's hold on us is far greater than man's hold on us could ever be. God's help gives the psalmist the confidence and ability to look triumphantly at his enemies. Resting in God's help and protection in our own lives leads us to look triumphantly upon our suffering. Suffering in this life will not prevail because of the mighty deliverance of the Lord.

The psalmist's testimony offers a lesson to those reading. In verses 8-9, he writes how we should go to the Lord for help and protection rather than man. As followers of Christ, it is far better to trust God than to trust man—to go to the Lord for refuge instead of man for refuge. Yet how often do we actually live out this truth? Seeking refuge and trust in man often takes priority over seeking refuge and trust in God. While other people can help us, they can never offer the complete help and protection the Lord provides. Man will fail us, but God never will. Let this encourage us to seek God for our security in all things.

The faithfulness of the Lord expands as Psalm 118 continues. Verses 10-14 describe the psalmist's success over his enemies because of the help of the Lord. Three times, he writes he conquered his enemies in the name of the Lord. This means the psalmist fought for God's honor and glory. Even when his enemies surrounded him, with the Lord's help, he prevailed over them.

Looking at this psalm through the eyes of Jesus, these verses can describe Jesus's experience before and on the cross. Jesus experienced crowds of people mocking, spitting, and beating Him. Christ most certainly felt what it was like to be surrounded by those against Him. But He also experienced what it was like for our sins to surround Him. On the cross, Jesus took the weight of our sin and shame. But sin and death would not prevail. By rising from the grave, Jesus destroyed the powers of darkness, declaring victory over them.

The shouts of the king's victory in verses 15-16 reflect the shouts of victory believers have in Christ. Jesus's victory over sin and death causes us to proclaim, "The Lord's right hand performs valiantly!" These words mirror the words of David in Psalm 108:13, who before battle confidently states, "With God we will perform valiantly." These are also our cries of victory because the battle has been won. Through Christ's death and resurrection, God has performed valiantly. Victory is ours because of Jesus. God's victory can also be seen in verses 17-18. Because the king in the psalm escaped death, he can declare victory. Verse 18 reflects the experience of Christ. Jesus may have died on the cross, but He did not stay dead. God did not give Him over to death but resurrected Him from the dead by His power.

Verses 19-24 describe the triumphant procession the king makes through Jerusalem after his victory. These verses describe the king's entrance through the city gates with praise to God. In verse 22, the psalmist writes how although enemies rejected him, he prevailed over them. Jesus uses this verse in Luke 20:17 to describe His future victory on the cross. Mankind may have rejected Christ, but God was still faithful to bring salvation through His death and resurrection. Because of His victory, Jesus is our cornerstone—the foundation upon which our faith is built.

The triumphant procession continues in verses 25-27 with the shouts of the people. The word "save us" is the word "Hosanna" in Hebrew. This was the same word the Jews cried as Jesus experienced His own triumphant procession through Jerusalem in Matthew 21:9. These cries of blessing turned to cries of hatred during Jesus's arrest (Matthew 27:20-23). However, even in their rejection, Jesus answered their desire for salvation through His death and resurrection. Like the festival sacrifice mentioned in verse 27, Jesus was nailed to the cross as the sacrifice in our place.

The good news of the gospel causes us to proclaim God's enduring, faithful love. The salvation we have received leads us to shout with praise over the victory of our great King. Our victory in Jesus gives us victory over our sins and sufferings. We can look triumphantly over both our personal sin and the sin of the world, knowing God will bring deliverance. As we await that day, we trust and rest in the salvation of our faithful God.

Our victory in Jesus

GIVES US VICTORY OVER OUR

SINS AND SUFFERINGS.

HOW DO YOU STRUGGLE WITH FEAR OF MAN OVER FEAR OF THE LORD? WHAT DOES IT LOOK LIKE
FOR YOU TO TRUST AND SEEK GOD FOR REFUGE INSTEAD OF OTHER PEOPLE?

_____

HOW ARE CHRIST'S GRACE AND MERCY DISPLAYED THROUGH HIS SACRIFICE ON THE CROSS?

_____

READ I PETER 2:1-10. HOW DO BELIEVERS REFLECT JESUS, THEIR CORNERSTONE?
HOW ARE WE TO LIVE IN LIGHT OF THIS TRUTH?

_____

God's Eternal and Faithful Word

READ PSALM 119

Psalm 119 is all about the Word of God. It speaks to the importance of God's Word and our need to obey God's Word. While Psalm 117 was the shortest psalm, Psalm 119 is the longest. Like Psalm 117, the length of this psalm may prompt us to skip over it, but if we do so, we miss out on treasured truth.

As readers, this psalm connects with us as the psalmist speaks to the reality of desiring to read God's Word while also being cast down. We, too, know what it is like to feel downcast and spiritually dry. The psalmist in Psalm 119 encourages us to continuously come before God's Word, even when we feel low, for in these moments, we need God's Word the most.

Psalm 119 is broken up into 22 stanzas, with eight lines in each stanza marked by a letter of the Hebrew alphabet. This type of structure is called an acrostic. Psalm 119 begins with the first letter of the Hebrew alphabet and ends with the last. Each stanza creatively focuses on a certain theme in relation to God's Word.

Throughout Psalm 119, the psalmist speaks to the importance of walking in God's Word. In the very first verse, the psalmist writes how those who walk according to God's instruction and seek to walk in His ways are happy. As believers, obeying God's Word brings us joy. Walking in the truth of God's Word causes us to experience the fullness of life given to us through Christ. Psalm 119 also teaches us the importance of treasuring God's Word. In fact, as we treasure God's Word, we will be led to obey God's Word. We treasure God's Word by rejoicing in, delighting in, and meditating upon God's Word (Psalm 119:14-16). We treasure what we adore. When we treasure God's Word, we make it a priority in our life. Continuously coming before and meditating upon God's Word keeps our hearts attuned to obey our heavenly Father.

As believers, we are also to behold God's Word. In verse 18, the psalmist asks God to open his eyes to see wondrous things from His Word. This is a great prayer to model in our own Scripture reading. God's Word has wonderful truths to discover, and through the Holy Spirit, God stands ready to help us discover them. Psalm 119 also teaches us how to come to God's Word when we are low. The psalmist honestly shares how he feels weary—as if his life is in the dust (verses 25 and 28). Yet the psalmist continues to come to God's Word, asking that God would use His Word to strengthen him and give him life. Times of sorrow are opportunities to move toward God's Word rather than away from it. When we are downcast, God's Word renews our hope, gives us joy, and sets our minds on the truth that encourages us. The psalmist speaks in verses 49-56 about how God's Word brought him comfort in affliction. Even in the darkest nights, he remembered God's name and sought to obey His Word. God's Word is a balm of comfort in times of pain. In moments of suffering, the truth of who God is and the promises of His Word uplift our souls.

Psalm 119 also teaches us how God gives us understanding for His Word. In verses 33-34, the psalmist asks God to help him understand the meaning and instruction of His Word. In our own personal Scripture reading, we are not alone when it comes to understanding God's Word. God has given us the Holy Spirit to help us glean from Scripture and to aid us when understanding Scripture is difficult. The psalmist also asks for help staying diligent in God's Word (verses 36-37). The psalmist asks God to turn his heart to God's decrees and to turn his eyes away from worthless things. Let us incorporate these prayers into our own lives by asking God to keep us focused on His Word above all.

God's Word also imparts wisdom. As we meditate upon God's instruction, we grow in wisdom (verse 98). No earthly wisdom compares to the wisdom of God's Word. Verse 105 reminds us how God's Word is a lamp that directs our paths. Because God's Word imparts wisdom, it gives us direction and keeps us from stumbling into the darkness of sin. As believers, we do not walk in darkness, for God's Word illuminates the path of life.

As believers, we also ought to long for God's Word. The psalmist describes in verse 131 how he opens his mouth and pants in longing over God's commands. When we recognize our need for God's Word, we will long for His Word. A parched mouth pants because it needs water. Taking in Scripture is like taking in gulps of water. Drinking deeply from the truth of God's Word saturates our soul. God's Word provides deep renewal. May our longing for this renewal lead us to His Word.

There are not enough words to describe all Psalm 119 has to teach us. As we journey through these stanzas, we are reminded that God's Word is the foundation of the Christian life. Without God's Word, we wander away from our primary source for knowing God and knowing ourselves. The psalmist's diligence to walk in God's commands encourages us to daily follow the Lord. Ultimately, our desire to obey God's Word stems from our understanding of the gospel. Our salvation is not just an entry point into heaven but the means for growing in Christlikeness. We respond to the gospel's good news by joyfully obeying the One who set us free from sin. We need God's Word to help us grow in the gospel and live out the gospel. God's Word is a treasure given to us by God Himself. May the beauty and wonder of Scripture lead us to daily seek His Word.

As we meditate upon God's instruction,

WE GROW IN WISDOM.

READ THROUGH PSALM 119, AND WRITE DOWN THE REFERENCES

THAT SPEAK TO EACH OF THESE THEMES.

DELIGHT	UNDERSTANDING	MEDITATION	PRAISE	OBEDIENCE

WHAT ARE SOME STRUGGLES YOU HAVE IN READING GOD'S WORD?

IN WHAT WAYS DOES THIS PSALM ENCOURAGE YOU IN THOSE STRUGGLES?

WHAT ARE SOME PRAYERS OF THE PSALMIST YOU CAN

INCORPORATE IN YOUR OWN PRAYERS?

A Prayer for Peace

READ PSALM 120

When we go on a journey, we can sometimes experience difficulty along the way. Instead of a smooth and easy trip, we can run into roadblocks, detours, and accidents. Because of these issues, getting to our destination can be discouraging. The subtitle for Psalm 120 is "a song of ascents." Israelite pilgrims sang these psalms as they journeyed to Jerusalem to celebrate feasts and festivals. These pilgrims had to journey through different lands, encountering people who did not follow the Lord along the way. In Psalm 120, the pilgrim expresses his distress over people who slander and despise peace. Even still, the pilgrim clings to truth and peace as he makes his way to the city of Jerusalem.

In verses 1-2, the psalmist prays for God's rescue. In these two verses, we learn the importance of prayer in times of distress. The deceitful people have caused the psalmist distress, and he calls out to the Lord for help. He not only calls out to the Lord, but he also receives a response. Have you experienced someone lying against you or to you? While we may not have experienced someone spreading lies about us, we all have experienced being lied to. We live in a broken world, which means there are people in our world speaking words that are opposite of the truth of God's Word. Hearing people around us speak lies can be extremely discouraging. Yet, these verses reveal what our first response should be in these moments: prayer. In times of distress, we have a God who hears and answers our prayers.

The psalmist may be in distress, but verses 3-4 reveal how he hopes in God's rescue, even in his distress. In verse 3, the psalmist asks what God's response to lying tongues is, and the psalmist gives the answers in verse 4. God does not allow deceitful people to go unpunished. Elsewhere in the book of Psalms, David writes, "You destroy those who speak lies; the Lord abhors the bloodthirsty and deceitful man" (Psalm 5:6, ESV). Psalm 120:4 explains how the deceitful man's fiery tongue is like a weapon of sharp arrows, yet his fiery tongue is met with burning charcoal from the Lord. Later, in the New Testament, James also describes the tongue as fire, writing how the tongue is a small part of the body that can have devastating effects when used unrighteously (James 3:5). Lying tongues are like fiery arrows—they destroy and burn those who hear them and receive them. Yet fiery tongues will not wage war forever. God's power will extinguish the flames of fiery tongues and punish them for their lies.

In the psalmist's distress, he can cling to the hope that God will provide rescue. Even if he must wait, he can trust the Lord will bring about justice. In our own lives, we can find peace knowing deceitful people will not go unpunished. God hears every sinful word that leaves their tongues and will punish them for their words. If people slander us, we do not need to retaliate but rest in the Lord's deliverance.

As the psalmist closes his song, he expresses his misery over being in the company of deceitful people. He mentions two places, Mesech and Kedar, to describe being among people who do not trust in the Lord. Being with these people who hate peace has led to the psalmist's distress. Even when he speaks for peace, the people only seek war. Verses 5-7 teach perseverance while waiting for God's rescue. The psalmist may be among people who seek destruction, but he remains committed to the truth. He does not follow the ways of the people by seeking war instead of peace or lies instead of truth. The psalmist remains committed to peace and truth.

As we wait for God to bring about deliverance from deceit, we must remain grounded in truth and peace. The enemy is the father of lies (John 8:44), but God is the father of truth (Numbers 23:19). We reflect the God of truth by being people committed to the truth. Daily, we are to remain rooted in God's Word. We also reflect Christ when we speak truth instead of lies. Colossians 3:9-10 tell us not to lie to one another since the salvation of Christ has replaced our old selves with a new self. Our new selves are being renewed in knowledge after the image of our Creator, which means as we grow in our walk with Christ, we will reflect His words and actions.

At times, we may struggle with controlling our tongues. In these moments, we have the sure promise of Christ's grace. Yet, the power of our words should remind us of the power of our gospel witness. The way we speak impacts our witness as believers. Let us ask for the Spirit's help in controlling our tongues so that we can speak words of life to others.

As believers, we are also called to be peacemakers. God is a God of peace. Just like we are to reflect the God of truth, so we are to reflect the God of peace. Even when the world seeks to wage war, we must seek to bring peace. We must not fight fire with fire, but we must speak words of grace and peace.

Like these pilgrims, we are all on a journey awaiting the ultimate city, the new heaven and the new earth. We have a marvelous destiny awaiting us, which makes the journey in between worth it. We may experience the distress of the broken world now, but this distress is temporary. As we wait for Christ to make all things new, may our feet remain fixed on the path of righteousness, firm in our faith.

As we wait for Christ to make all things new, MAY OUR FEET REMAIN FIXED ON THE PATH OF RIGHTEOUSNESS, FIRM IN OUR FAITH.

WHAT LIES HAVE YOU HEARD THE WORLD SPEAK AND BELIEVE?
WHAT ARE SOME LIES YOU HAVE BELIEVED YOURSELF?

———————————————

WHY IS IT IMPORTANT TO GROUND OUR TRUTH IN GOD'S WORD?
HOW CAN YOU DAILY GROUND YOURSELF IN THE WORD OF GOD?

———————————————

HOW CAN YOU REMAIN COMMITTED TO PEACE AND
TRUTH IN A WORLD THAT SEEKS THE OPPOSITE?

———————————————

Scripture Memory

LORD, YOUR WORD IS FOREVER; IT IS FIRMLY
FIXED IN HEAVEN. YOUR FAITHFULNESS IS
FOR ALL GENERATIONS; YOU ESTABLISHED
THE EARTH, AND IT STANDS FIRM.

Psalm 119:89-90

Week Six Reflection

SUMMARIZE THE MAIN POINTS FROM THIS WEEK'S SCRIPTURE READINGS.

WHAT DID YOU OBSERVE FROM THIS WEEK'S PASSAGES ABOUT GOD AND HIS CHARACTER?

WHAT DO THIS WEEK'S PASSAGES REVEAL ABOUT THE CONDITION OF MANKIND AND YOURSELF?

Read Psalms 116-120

HOW DO THESE PASSAGES POINT TO THE GOSPEL?

HOW SHOULD YOU RESPOND TO THESE PASSAGES? WHAT SPECIFIC
ACTION STEPS CAN YOU TAKE THIS WEEK TO APPLY THEM IN YOUR LIFE?

WRITE A PRAYER IN RESPONSE TO YOUR STUDY OF GOD'S WORD. ADORE GOD FOR WHO HE IS,
CONFESS SINS HE REVEALED IN YOUR OWN LIFE, ASK HIM TO EMPOWER YOU TO WALK IN OBE-
DIENCE, AND PRAY FOR ANYONE WHO COMES TO MIND AS YOU STUDY.

Oh, Praise the Lord (Psalm 117)

CHARLES W. NAYLOR

Oh, praise the Lord, all ye nations!
Praise Him, all ye people!
For His merciful kindness is great toward us,
And the truth of the Lord endureth forever;
Praise ye the Lord!

REFRAIN:

Praise Him, praise Him!
Praise ye the Lord!
Praise Him, praise Him!
Praise ye the Lord!

Oh, praise the Lord, all ye nations!
Praise Him for His goodness;
For He saveth His people from all their sins,
And preserveth the souls of all who will trust Him;
Praise ye the Lord!

REFRAIN

Oh, praise the Lord, all ye nations!
He is strong and mighty;
For He keepeth our steps that we shall not fall,
And delivers His saints from all their temptations;
Praise ye the Lord!

REFRAIN

Oh, praise the Lord, all ye nations!
For His love unfailing;
He doth tenderly lead in the path of peace,
And His name is a refuge from the oppressor;
Praise ye the Lord!

REFRAIN

OUR GOD IS WORTHY

TO BE PRAISED.

Hallelujah!

What is the Gospel?

THANK YOU FOR READING AND ENJOYING THIS STUDY WITH US! WE ARE ABUNDANTLY GRATEFUL FOR THE WORD OF GOD, THE INSTRUCTION WE GLEAN FROM IT, AND THE EVER-GROWING UNDERSTANDING IT PROVIDES FOR US OF GOD'S CHARACTER. WE ARE ALSO THANKFUL THAT SCRIPTURE CONTINUALLY POINTS TO ONE THING IN INNUMERABLE WAYS: THE GOSPEL.

We remember our brokenness when we read about the fall of Adam and Eve in the garden of Eden (Genesis 3), where sin entered into a perfect world and maimed it. We remember the necessity that something innocent must die to pay for our sin when we read about the atoning sacrifices in the Old Testament. We read that we have all sinned and fallen short of the glory of God (Romans 3:23) and that the penalty for our brokenness, the wages of our sin, is death (Romans 6:23). We all need grace and mercy, but most importantly, we all need a Savior.

We consider the goodness of God when we realize that He did not plan to leave us in this dire state. We see His promise to buy us back from the clutches of sin and death in Genesis 3:15. And we see that promise accomplished with Jesus Christ on the cross. Jesus Christ knew no sin yet became sin so that we might become righteous through His sacrifice (2 Corinthians 5:21). Jesus was tempted in every way that we are and lived sinlessly. He was reviled yet still yielded Himself for our sake, that we may have life abundant in Him. Jesus lived the perfect life that we could not live and died the death that we deserved.

The gospel is profound yet simple. There are many mysteries in it that we will never understand this side of heaven, but there is still overwhelming weight to its implications in this life. The gospel tells of our sinfulness and God's goodness and a gracious gift that compels a response. We are saved by grace through faith, which means that we rest with faith in the grace that Jesus Christ displayed on the cross (Ephesians 2:8-9). We cannot save ourselves from our brokenness or do any amount of good works to merit God's favor. Still, we can have faith that what Jesus accomplished in His death, burial, and resurrection was more than enough for our salvation and our eternal delight. When we accept God, we are commanded to die to ourselves and our sinful desires and live a life worthy of the calling we have received (Ephesians 4:1). The gospel compels us to be sanctified, and in so doing, we are conformed to the likeness of Christ Himself. This is hope. This is redemption. This is the gospel.

SCRIPTURES TO REFERENCE:

GENESIS 3:15

I will put hostility between you and the woman, and between your offspring and her offspring. He will strike your head, and you will strike his heel.

ROMANS 3:23

For all have sinned and fall short of the glory of God.

ROMANS 6:23

For the wages of sin is death, but the gift of God is eternal life in Christ Jesus our Lord.

2 CORINTHIANS 5:21

He made the one who did not know sin to be sin for us, so that in him we might become the righteousness of God.

EPHESIANS 2:8-9

For you are saved by grace through faith, and this is not from yourselves; it is God's gift—not from works, so that no one can boast.

EPHESIANS 4:1-3

Therefore I, the prisoner in the Lord, urge you to walk worthy of the calling you have received, with all humility and gentleness, with patience, bearing with one another in love, making every effort to keep the unity of the Spirit through the bond of peace.

Thank you for studying
God's Word with us!